DOVER·THRIFT·EDITIONS

Pre-Raphaelite Poetry
An Anthology

Edited by
PAUL NEGRI

DOVER PUBLICATIONS, INC.
Mineola, New York

DOVER THRIFT EDITIONS

GENERAL EDITOR: PAUL NEGRI

EDITOR OF THIS VOLUME: THOMAS CRAWFORD

Bibliographical Note

Pre-Raphaelite Poetry: An Anthology is a new work, first published by Dover Publications, Inc., in 2003.

Library of Congress Cataloging-in-Publication Data

Pre-Raphaelite poetry : an anthology / edited by Paul Negri.
       p. cm. (Dover thrift editions)
   ISBN 0-486-42448-0 (pbk.)
    1. English poetry—19th century. 2. Pre-Raphaelitism—Poetry. I. Negri, Paul.

PR1223 .P66 2003
821'.808—dc21   2002034828

Manufactured in the United States of America
Dover Publications, Inc., 31 East 2nd Street, Mineola, N.Y. 11501

Note

BEGUN by a small group of English painters (Dante Gabriel Rossetti, Holman Hunt, John Everett Millais and others) in 1848, the pre-Raphaelite Brotherhood urged artists to reject academicism and return to the direct and uncomplicated depiction of nature found in Italian painting before Raphael, i.e. before the heyday of the Italian High Renaissance. Although the movement itself was short-lived, the Brotherhood exercised a powerful influence on subsequent painting, as well as on decorative arts and literature.

In the literary sphere the poetry of the Pre-Raphaelites was essentially elegiac, suffused with melancholy, etherealized passion, unsatisfied longing, and loss. It often revealed a conscious medievalism, and was frequently imbued with an overall religious and moralizing tone. Working within the precepts of the movement, such poets as Dante Gabriel Rossetti and Christina Rossetti, William Morris, George Meredith and Algernon Charles Swinburne produced sensuous, symbolic narrative verse, rich in pictorial detail and moody mysticism. Strongly influenced by Robert Browning, the Pre-Raphaelites in turn had a major impact on the Aesthetic and Decadent movements of the late Victorian era, evidenced in the work of such writers as Ernest Dowson, Walter Pater, and Oscar Wilde. Pre-Raphaelite ideas also affected the verse of Gerard Manley Hopkins and William Butler Yeats.

Often, Pre-Raphaelite poetry dealt with the unattainable and the melancholic. As Anthony H. Harrison points out in *Christina Rossetti in Context* (University of North Carolina Press, 1988), Pre-Raphaelite love poetry "usually depicts desires and pleasures of the flesh only in order ultimately to expose their futility except as passports to a superior and transcendent ideal realm and as inspirations for art, in which the torturous ardors of human passion come most attractively to fruition." The poetry "cultivates a tone of languorous melancholy, fully exploiting the elegiac potential of its materials, and is frequently described by contemporary reviewers as 'morbid.'"

In 1871, one of those reviewers fiercely attacked the Brotherhood. In an article entitled "The Fleshly School of Poetry" in the *Contemporary Review*, Robert Buchanan castigated the work of Rossetti and his contemporaries, in particular that of Swinburne, for its "morbid deviation from the healthy forms of life." He further decried the poets' "weary wasting, yet exquisite sensuality; nothing virile, nothing tender, nothing completely sane; a superfluity of extreme sensibility." Both Rossetti and Swinburne replied to Buchanan's criticisms in print, but Rossetti was never the same afterward, as the criticism exacerbated his already depressed state.

Despite the criticism of Buchanan and others, the Pre-Raphaelite sensibility has survived and flourished, and continues to influence artists and writers today. The Pre-Raphaelite interest in the medieval, in the psychological mind, in symbolism, in a new realism, had a profound impact on the history and evolution of art and poetry. This anthology contains a rich selection of works by the major Pre-Raphaelite poets, revealing the originality, purity of vision, and technical facility of this influential school of writers.

Contents

Selections from The House of Life:

Christina Rossetti

Contents

DANTE GABRIEL ROSSETTI
(1828–1882)

One of the founders of the Pre-Raphaelite Brotherhood (with Holman Hunt and John Everett Millais) in 1848, Dante Gabriel Rossetti was both a painter and a poet. In both genres, he strove to achieve the Pre-Raphaelite aim of encouraging "an entire adherence to the simplicity of nature." Characterized by a certain opulence and sensuality, which brought critical attacks in his day, Rossetti's poetry is nevertheless admired for its purity and lyricism, richness and vividness of detail, mysticism, fantasy, and frequent use of the modified ballad form. His 101-sonnet sequence, *The House of Life*, selections from which appear here, contains some of the finest sonnets of the period.

The Blessed Damozel

The blessed damozel leaned out
   From the gold bar of Heaven;
Her eyes were deeper than the depth
   Of waters stilled at even;
She had three lilies in her hand,
   And the stars in her hair were seven.

Her robe, ungirt from clasp to hem,
   No wrought flowers did adorn,
But a white rose of Mary's gift,
   For service meetly worn;
Her hair that lay along her back
   Was yellow like ripe corn.

Herseemed she scarce had been a day
    One of God's choristers;
The wonder was not yet quite gone
    From that still look of hers;
Albeit, to them she left, her day
    Had counted as ten years.

(To one, it is ten years of years.
    . . . Yet now, and in this place,
Surely she leaned o'er me—her hair
    Fell all about my face. . . .
Nothing: the autumn-fall of leaves.
    The whole year sets apace.)

It was the rampart of God's house
    That she was standing on;
By God built over the sheer depth
    The which is Space begun;
So high, that looking downward thence
    She scarce could see the sun.

It lies in Heaven, across the flood
    Of ether, as a bridge.
Beneath, the tides of day and night
    With flame and darkness ridge
The void, as low as where this earth
    Spins like a fretful midge.

Around her, lovers, newly met
    'Mid deathless love's acclaims,
Spoke evermore among themselves
    Their heart-remembered names;
And the souls mounting up to God
    Went by her like thin flames.

And still she bowed herself and stooped
    Out of the circling charm;
Until her bosom must have made
    The bar she leaned on warm,
And the lilies lay as if asleep
    Along her bended arm.

From the fixed place of Heaven she saw
   Time like a pulse shake fierce
Through all the worlds. Her gaze still strove
   Within the gulf to pierce
Its path; and now she spoke as when
   The stars sang in their spheres.

The sun was gone now; the curled moon
   Was like a little feather
Fluttering far down the gulf; and now
   She spoke through the still weather.
Her voice was like the voice the stars
   Had when they sang together.

(Ah sweet! Even now, in that bird's song,
   Strove not her accents there,
Fain to be hearkened? When those bells
   Possessed the mid-day air,
Strove not her steps to reach my side
   Down all the echoing stair?)

"I wish that he were come to me,
   For he will come," she said.
"Have I not prayed in Heaven?—on earth,
   Lord, Lord, has he not pray'd?
Are not two prayers a perfect strength?
   And shall I feel afraid?

"When round his head the aureole clings,
   And he is clothed in white,
I'll take his hand and go with him
   To the deep wells of light;
As unto a stream we will step down,
   And bathe there in God's sight.

"We two will stand beside that shrine,
   Occult, withheld, untrod,
Whose lamps are stirred continually
   With prayer sent up to God;
And see our old prayers, granted, melt
   Each like a little cloud.

"We two will lie i' the shadow of
    That living mystic tree
Within whose secret growth the Dove
    Is sometimes felt to be,
While every leaf that His plumes touch
    Saith His Name audibly.

"And I myself will teach to him,
    I myself, lying so,
The songs I sing here; which his voice
    Shall pause in, hushed and slow,
And find some knowledge at each pause,
    Or some new thing to know."

(Alas! we two, we two, thou say'st!
    Yea, one wast thou with me
That once of old. But shall God lift
    To endless unity
The soul whose likeness with thy soul
    Was but its love for thee?)

"We two," she said, "will seek the groves
    Where the lady Mary is,
With her five handmaidens, whose names
    Are five sweet symphonies,
Cecily, Gertrude, Magdalen,
    Margaret and Rosalys.

"Circlewise sit they, with bound locks
    And foreheads garlanded;
Into the fine cloth white like flame
    Weaving the golden thread,
To fashion the birth-robes for them
    Who are just born, being dead.

"He shall fear, haply, and be dumb;
    Then will I lay my cheek
To his, and tell about our love,
    Not once abashed or weak:
And the dear Mother will approve
    My pride, and let me speak.

"Herself shall bring us, hand in hand,
　　To Him round whom all souls
Kneel, the clear-ranged unnumbered heads
　　Bowed with their aureoles:
And angels meeting us shall sing
　　To their citherns and citoles.

"There will I ask of Christ the Lord
　　Thus much for him and me:—
Only to live as once on earth
　　With Love,—only to be,
As then awhile, for ever now
　　Together, I and he."

　She gazed and listened and then said,
　　　Less sad of speech than mild,—
　"All this is when he comes." She ceased.
　　　The light thrilled towards her, fill'd
　With angels in strong level flight.
　　　Her eyes prayed, and she smil'd.

　(I saw her smile.) But soon their path
　　　Was vague in distant spheres:
　And then she cast her arms along
　　　The golden barriers,
　And laid her face between her hands,
　　　And wept. (I heard her tears.)

My Sister's Sleep

She fell asleep on Christmas Eve.
　At length the long-ungranted shade
　Of weary eyelids overweigh'd
The pain nought else might yet relieve.

Our mother, who had leaned all day
　Over the bed from chime to chime,
　Then raised herself for the first time,
And as she sat her down, did pray.

Her little work-table was spread
   With work to finish. For the glare
   Made by her candle, she had care
To work some distance from the bed.

Without, there was a cold moon up,
   Of winter radiance sheer and thin;
   The hollow halo it was in
Was like an icy crystal cup.

Through the small room, with subtle sound
   Of flame, by vents the fireshine drove
   And reddened. In its dim alcove
The mirror shed a clearness round.

I had been sitting up some nights,
   And my tired mind felt weak and blank;
   Like a sharp strengthening wine it drank
The stillness and the broken lights.

Twelve struck. That sound, by dwindling years
   Heard in each hour, crept off; and then
   The ruffled silence spread again,
Like water that a pebble stirs.

Our mother rose from where she sat:
   Her needles, as she laid them down,
   Met lightly, and her silken gown
Settled: no other noise than that.

"Glory unto the Newly Born!"
   So, as said angels, she did say:
   Because we were in Christmas Day,
Though it would still be long till morn.

Just then in the room over us
   There was a pushing back of chairs,
   As some who had sat unawares
So late, now heard the hour, and rose.

With anxious softly-stepping haste
   Our mother went where Margaret lay,

Fearing the sounds o'erhead—should they
Have broken her long watched-for rest!

She stooped an instant, calm, and turned;
   But suddenly turned back again;
   And all her features seemed in pain
With woe, and her eyes gazed and yearned.

For my part, I but hid my face,
   And held my breath, and spoke no word:
   There was none spoken; but I heard
The silence for a little space.

Our mother bowed herself and wept:
   And both my arms fell, and I said,
   "God knows I knew that she was dead."
And there, all white, my sister slept.

Then kneeling, upon Christmas morn
   A little after twelve o'clock,
   We said, ere the first quarter struck,
"Christ's blessing on the newly born!"

The Portrait

This is her picture as she was:
   It seems a thing to wonder on,
As though mine image in the glass
   Should tarry when myself am gone.
I gaze until she seems to stir,—
Until mine eyes almost aver
   That now, even now, the sweet lips part
   To breathe the words of the sweet heart:—
And yet the earth is over her.

Alas! even such the thin-drawn ray
   That makes the prison-depths more rude,—
The drip of water night and day
   Giving a tongue to solitude.
Yet only this, of love's whole prize,
Remains; save what in mournful guise
   Takes counsel with my soul alone,—

Save what is secret and unknown,
Below the earth, above the skies.

In painting her I shrined her face
   'Mid mystic trees, where light falls in
Hardly at all; a covert place
   Where you might think to find a din
Of doubtful talk, and a live flame
Wandering, and many a shape whose name
   Not itself knoweth, and old dew,
   And your own footsteps meeting you,
And all things going as they came.

A deep dim wood; and there she stands
   As in that wood that day: for so
Was the still movement of her hands
   And such the pure line's gracious flow.
And passing fair the type must seem,
Unknown the presence and the dream.
   'Tis she: though of herself, alas!
   Less than her shadow on the grass
Or than her image in the stream.

That day we met there, I and she
   One with the other all alone;
And we were blithe; yet memory
   Saddens those hours, as when the moon
Looks upon daylight. And with her
I stooped to drink the spring-water,
   Athirst where other waters sprang:
   And where the echo is, she sang,—
My soul another echo there.

But when that hour my soul won strength
   For words whose silence wastes and kills,
Dull raindrops smote us, and at length
   Thundered the heat within the hills.
That eve I spoke those words again
Beside the pelted window-pane;
   And there she hearkened what I said,
   With under-glances that surveyed
The empty pastures blind with rain.

Next day the memories of these things,
    Like leaves through which a bird has flown,
Still vibrated with Love's warm wings;
    Till I must make them all my own
And paint this picture. So, 'twixt ease
Of talk and sweet long silences,
    She stood among the plants in bloom
    At windows of a summer room,
To feign the shadow of the trees.

And as I wrought, while all above
    And all around was fragrant air,
In the sick burthen of my love
    It seemed each sun-thrilled blossom there
Beat like a heart among the leaves.
O heart that never beats nor heaves,
    In that one darkness lying still,
    What now to thee my love's great will
Or the fine web the sunshine weaves?

For now doth daylight disavow
    Those days—nought left to see or hear.
Only in solemn whispers now
    At night-time these things reach mine ear;
When the leaf-shadows at a breath
Shrink in the road, and all the heath,
    Forest and water, far and wide,
    In limpid starlight glorified,
Lie like the mystery of death.

Last night at last I could have slept,
    And yet delayed my sleep till dawn,
Still wandering. Then it was I wept:
    For unawares I came upon
Those glades where once she walked with me,
And as I stood there suddenly,
    All wan with traversing the night,
    Upon the desolate verge of light
Yearned loud the iron-bosomed sea.

Even so, where Heaven holds breath and hears
    The beating heart of Love's own breast,—

Where round the secret of all spheres
   All angels lay their wings to rest,—
How shall my soul stand rapt and awed,
When, by the new birth borne abroad
   Throughout the music of the suns,
   It enters in her soul at once
And knows the silence there for God!

Here with her face doth memory sit
   Meanwhile, and wait the day's decline,
Till other eyes shall look from it,
   Eyes of the spirit's Palestine,
Even than the old gaze tenderer:
While hopes and aims long lost with her
   Stand round her image side by side,
   Like tombs of pilgrims that have died
About the Holy Sepulchre.

Ave

Mother of the Fair Delight,
Thou handmaid perfect in God's sight,
Now sitting fourth beside the Three,
Thyself a woman-Trinity,—
Being a daughter born to God,
Mother of Christ from stall to rood,
And wife unto the Holy Ghost:—
Oh when our need is uttermost,
Think that to such as death may strike
Thou once wert sister sisterlike!
Thou headstone of humanity,
Groundstone of the great Mystery,
Fashioned like us, yet more than we!

   Mind'st thou not (when June's heavy breath
Warmed the long days in Nazareth,)
That eve thou didst go forth to give
Thy flowers some drink that they might live
One faint night more amid the sands?
Far off the trees were as pale wands
Against the fervid sky: the sea
Sighed further off eternally
As human sorrow sighs in sleep.

Then suddenly the awe grew deep,
As of a day to which all days
Were footsteps in God's secret ways:
Until a folding sense, like prayer,
Which is, as God is, everywhere,
Gathered about thee; and a voice
Spake to thee without any noise,
Being of the silence:—"Hail," it said,
"Thou that art highly favourèd;
The Lord is with thee here and now;
Blessed among all women thou."

   Ah! knew'st thou of the end, when first
That Babe was on thy bosom nurs'd?—
Or when He tottered round thy knee
Did thy great sorrow dawn on thee?—
And through His boyhood, year by year
Eating with Him the Passover,
Didst thou discern confusedly
That holier sacrament, when He,
The bitter cup about to quaff,
Should break the bread and eat thereof?—
Or came not yet the knowledge, even
Till on some day forecast in Heaven
His feet passed through thy door to press
Upon His Father's business?—
Or still was God's high secret kept?

   Nay, but I think the whisper crept
Like growth through childhood. Work and play,
Things common to the course of day,
Awed thee with meanings unfulfill'd;
And all through girlhood, something still'd
Thy senses like the birth of light,
When thou hast trimmed thy lamp at night
Or washed thy garments in the stream;
To whose white bed had come the dream
That He was thine and thou wast His
Who feeds among the field-lilies.
O solemn shadow of the end
In that wise spirit long contain'd!
O awful end! and those unsaid
Long years when It was Finishèd!

Mind'st thou not (when the twilight gone
Left darkness in the house of John,)
Between the naked window-bars
That spacious vigil of the stars?—
For thou, a watcher even as they,
Wouldst rise from where throughout the day
Thou wroughtest raiment for His poor;
And, finding the fixed terms endure
Of day and night which never brought
Sounds of His coming chariot,
Wouldst lift through cloud-waste unexplor'd
Those eyes which said, "How long, O Lord?"
Then that disciple whom He loved,
Well heeding, haply would be moved
To ask thy blessing in His name;
And that one thought in both, the same
Though silent, then would clasp ye round
To weep together,—tears long bound,
Sick tears of patience, dumb and slow.
Yet, "Surely I come quickly,"—so
He said, from life and death gone home.
Amen: even so, Lord Jesus, come!

But oh! what human tongue can speak
That day when Michael came to break
From the tir'd spirit, like a veil,
Its covenant with Gabriel
Endured at length unto the end?
What human thought can apprehend
That mystery of motherhood
When thy Beloved at length renew'd
The sweet communion severèd,—
His left hand underneath thine head
And His right hand embracing thee?—
Lo! He was thine, and this is He!

Soul, is it Faith, or Love, or Hope,
That lets me see her standing up
Where the light of the Throne is bright?
Unto the left, unto the right,
The cherubim, succinct, conjoint,
Float inward to a golden point,
And from between the seraphim
The glory issues for a hymn.

O Mary Mother, be not loth
To listen,—thou whom the stars clothe,
Who seëst and mayst not be seen!
Here us at last, O Mary Queen!
Into our shadow bend thy face,
Bowing thee from the secret place
O Mary Virgin, full of grace!

Autumn Song

Know'st thou not at the fall of the leaf
How the heart feels a languid grief
    Laid on it for a covering,
     And how sleep seems a goodly thing
In Autumn at the fall of the leaf?

And how the swift beat of the brain
Falters because it is in vain,
    In Autumn at the fall of the leaf
     Knowest thou not? and how the chief
Of joys seems—not to suffer pain?

Know'st thou not at the fall of the leaf
How the soul feels like a dried sheaf
    Bound up at length for harvesting,
     And how death seems a comely thing
In Autumn at the fall of the leaf?

Place de la Bastille, Paris

How dear the sky has been above this place!
   Small treasures of this sky that we see here
   Seen weak through prison-bars from year to year;
Eyed with a painful prayer upon God's grace
To save, and tears that stayed along the face
   Lifted at sunset. Yea, how passing dear,
   Those nights when through the bars a wind left clear
The heaven, and moonlight soothed the limpid space!

So was it, till one night the secret kept
   Safe in low vault and stealthy corridor
    Was blown abroad on gospel-tongues of flame.

O ways of God, mysterious evermore!
How many on this spot have cursed and wept
    That all might stand here now and own Thy Name.

For a Venetian Pastoral

BY GIORGIONE

(In the Louvre)

Water, for anguish of the solstice:—nay,
  But dip the vessel slowly,—nay, but lean
  And hark how at its verge the wave sighs in
Reluctant. Hush! beyond all depth away
The heat lies silent at the brink of day:
  Now the hand trails upon the viol-string
  That sobs, and the brown faces cease to sing,
Sad with the whole of pleasure. Whither stray
Her eyes now, from whose mouth the slim pipes creep
  And leave it pouting, while the shadowed grass
    Is cool against her naked side? Let be:—
Say nothing now unto her lest she weep,
  Nor name this ever. Be it as it was,—
    Life touching lips with Immortality.

The Card-Dealer

Could you not drink her gaze like wine?
  Yet though its splendour swoon
Into the silence languidly
  As a tune into a tune,
Those eyes unravel the coiled night
  And know the stars at noon.

The gold that's heaped beside her hand,
  In truth rich prize it were;
And rich the dreams that wreathe her brows
  With magic stillness there;
And he were rich who should unwind
  That woven golden hair.

Around her, where she sits, the dance
  Now breathes its eager heat;

And not more lightly or more true
 Fall there the dancers' feet
Than fall her cards on the bright board
 As 'twere a heart that beat.

Her fingers let them softly through,
 Smooth polished silent things;
And each one as it falls reflects
 In swift light-shadowings,
Blood-red and purple, green and blue,
 The great eyes of her rings.

Whom plays she with? With thee, who lov'st
 Those gems upon her hand;
With me, who search her secret brows;
 With all men, bless'd or bann'd.
We play together, she and we,
 Within a vain strange land:

A land without any order,—
 Day even as night, (one saith,)—
Where who lieth down ariseth not
 Nor the sleeper awakeneth;
A land of darkness as darkness itself
 And of the shadow of death.

What be her cards, you ask? Even these:—
 The heart, that doth but crave
More, having fed; the diamond,
 Skilled to make base seem brave;
The club, for smiting in the dark;
 The spade, to dig a grave.

And do you ask what game she plays?
 With me 'tis lost or won;
With thee it is playing still; with him
 It is not well begun;
But 'tis a game she plays with all
 Beneath the sway o' the sun.

Thou seest the card that falls,—she knows
 The card that followeth:
Her game in thy tongue is called Life,

As ebbs thy daily breath:
When she shall speak, thou'lt learn her tongue
And know she calls it Death.

The Sea-Limits

Consider the sea's listless chime:
    Time's self it is, made audible,—
    The murmur of the earth's own shell.
Secret continuance sublime
    Is the sea's end: our sight may pass
    No furlong further. Since time was,
This sound hath told the lapse of time.

No quiet, which is death's,—it hath
    The mournfulness of ancient life,
    Enduring always at dull strife.
As the world's heart of rest and wrath,
    Its painful pulse is in the sands.
    Last utterly, the whole sky stands,
Grey and not known, along its path.

Listen alone beside the sea,
    Listen alone among the woods;
    Those voices of twin solitudes
Shall have one sound alike to thee:
    Hark where the murmurs of thronged men
    Surge and sink back and surge again,—
Still the one voice of wave and tree.

Gather a shell from the strown beach
    And listen at its lips: they sigh
    The same desire and mystery,
The echo of the whole sea's speech.
    And all mankind is thus at heart
    Not anything but what thou art:
And Earth, Sea, Man, are all in each.

A Young Fir-Wood

These little firs to-day are things
    To clasp into a giant's cap,
    Or fans to suit his lady's lap.

From many winters many springs
    Shall cherish them in strength and sap
    Till they be marked upon the map,
A wood for the wind's wanderings.

All seed is in the sower's hands:
    And what at first was trained to spread
    Its shelter for some single head,—
'Yea, even such fellowship of wands,—
    May hide the sunset, and the shade
    Of its great multitude be laid
Upon the earth and elder sands.

The Mirror

She knew it not:—most perfect pain
    To learn: this too she knew not. Strife
      For me, calm hers, as from the first.
      'Twas but another bubble burst
    Upon the curdling draught of life,—
My silent patience mine again.

As who, of forms that crowd unknown
    Within a distant mirror's shade,
      Deems such an one himself, and makes
      Some sign—but when the image shakes
    No whit, he finds his thought betray'd,
And must seek elsewhere for his own.

A Match with the Moon

Weary already, weary miles to-night
    I walked for bed: and so, to get some ease,
    I dogged the flying moon with similes.
And like a wisp she doubled on my sight
In ponds; and caught in tree-tops like a kite;
    And in a globe of film all liquorish
    Swam full-faced like a silly silver fish;—
Last like a bubble shot the welkin's height
Where my road turned, and got behind me, and sent
    My wizened shadow craning round at me,
    And jeered, "So, step the measure,—one two three!"—

And if I faced on her, looked innocent.
But just at parting, halfway down a dell,
She kissed me for good-night. So you'll not tell.

Sudden Light

I have been here before,
    But when or how I cannot tell:
I know the grass beyond the door,
    The sweet keen smell,
The sighing sound, the lights around the shore.

You have been mine before, —
    How long ago I may not know:
But just when at that swallow's soar
    Your neck turned so,
Some veil did fall, — I knew it all of yore.

Has this been thus before?
    And shall not thus time's eddying flight
Still with our lives our love restore
    In death's despite,
And day and night yield one delight once more?

On the *Vita Nuova* of Dante

As he that loves oft looks on the dear form
    And guesses how it grew to womanhood,
    And gladly would have watched the beauties bud
And the mild fire of precious life wax warm:
So I, long bound within the threefold charm
    Of Dante's love sublimed to heavenly mood,
    Had marvelled, touching his Beatitude,
How grew such presence from man's shameful swarm.

At length within this book I found portrayed
    Newborn that Paradisal Love of his,
And simple like a child; with whose clear aid
    I understood. To such a child as this,
Christ, charging well His chosen ones, forbade
    Offence: "for lo! of such my kingdom is."

Penumbra

I did not look upon her eyes,
(Though scarcely seen, with no surprise,
'Mid many eyes a single look,)
Because they should not gaze rebuke,
At night, from stars in sky and brook.

I did not take her by the hand,
(Though little was to understand
From touch of hand all friends might take,)
Because it should not prove a flake
Burnt in my palm to boil and ache.

I did not listen to her voice,
(Though none had noted, where at choice
All might rejoice in listening,)
Because no such a thing should cling
In the wood's moan at evening.

I did not cross her shadow once,
(Though from the hollow west the sun's
Last shadow runs along so far,)
Because in June it should not bar
My ways, at noon when fevers are.

They told me she was sad that day,
(Though wherefore tell what love's soothsay,
Sooner than they, did register?)
And my heart leapt and wept to her,
And yet I did not speak nor stir.

So shall the tongues of the sea's foam
(Though many voices therewith come
From drowned hope's home to cry to me,)
Bewail one hour the more, when sea
And wind are one with memory.

The Honeysuckle

I plucked a honeysuckle where
    The hedge on high is quick with thorn,
    And climbing for the prize, was torn,
And fouled my feet in quag-water;

And by the thorns and by the wind
   The blossom that I took was thinn'd,
And yet I found it sweet and fair.

Thence to a richer growth I came,
   Where, nursed in mellow intercourse,
   The honeysuckles sprang by scores,
Not harried like my single stem,
   All virgin lamps of scent and dew.
   So from my hand that first I threw,
Yet plucked not any more of them.

Sister Helen

"Why did you melt your waxen man,
                  Sister Helen?
To-day is the third since you began."
"The time was long, yet the time ran,
                  Little brother."
            (O Mother, Mary Mother,
Three days to-day, between Hell and Heaven!)

"But if you have done your work aright,
                  Sister Helen?
You'll let me play, for you said I might."
"Be very still in your play to-night,
                  Little brother."
            (O Mother, Mary Mother,
Third night, to-night, between Hell and Heaven!)

"You said it must melt ere vesper-bell,
                  Sister Helen;
If now it be molten, all is well."
"Even so,—nay, peace! you cannot tell,
                  Little brother."
            (O Mother, Mary Mother,
O what is this, between Hell and Heaven?)

"Oh the waxen knave was plump to-day,
                  Sister Helen;

How like dead folk he has dropped away!"
"Nay now, of the dead what can you say,
                    Little brother?"
                    (O Mother, Mary Mother,
What of the dead, between Hell and Heaven?)

"See, see, the sunken pile of wood,
                    Sister Helen,
Shines through the thinned wax red as blood!"
"Nay now, when looked you yet on blood,
                    Little brother?"
                    (O Mother, Mary Mother,
How pale she is, between Hell and Heaven!)

"Now close your eyes, for they're sick and sore,
                    Sister Helen,
And I'll play without the gallery door."
"Aye, let me rest,—I'll lie on the floor,
                    Little brother."
                    (O Mother, Mary Mother,
What rest to-night, between Hell and Heaven?)

"Here high up in the balcony,
                    Sister Helen,
The morn flies face to face with me."
"Aye, look and say whatever you see,
                    Little brother."
                    (O Mother, Mary Mother,
What sight to-night, between Hell and Heaven?)

"Outside it's merry in the wind's wake,
                    Sister Helen;
In the shaken trees the chill stars shake."
"Hush, heard you a horse-tread as you spake,
                    Little brother?"
                    (O Mother, Mary Mother,
What sound to-night, between Hell and Heaven?).

"I hear a horse-tread, and I see,
                    Sister Helen,
Three horsemen that ride terribly."

"Little brother, whence come the three,
                    Little brother?"
              (O Mother, Mary Mother,
Whence should they come, between Hell and Heaven?)

"They come by the hill-verge from Boyne Bar,
                    Sister Helen,
And one draws nigh, but two are afar."
"Look, look, do you know them who they are,
                    Little brother?"
              (O Mother, Mary Mother,
Who should they be, between Hell and Heaven?)

"Oh, it's Keith of Eastholm rides so fast,
                    Sister Helen,
For I know the white mane on the blast."
"The hour has come, has come at last,
                    Little brother!"
              (O Mother, Mary Mother,
Her hour at last, between Hell and Heaven!)

"He has made a sign and called Halloo!
                    Sister Helen,
And he says that he would speak with you."
"Oh tell him I fear the frozen dew,
                    Little brother."
              (O Mother, Mary Mother,
Why laughs she thus, between Hell and Heaven?)

"The wind is loud, but I hear him cry,
                    Sister Helen,
That Keith of Ewern's like to die."
"And he and thou, and thou and I,
                    Little brother."
              (O Mother, Mary Mother,
And they and we, between Hell and Heaven!)

"Three days ago, on his marriage-morn,
                    Sister Helen,
He sickened, and lies since then forlorn."
"For bridegroom's side is the bride a thorn,
                    Little brother?"

(O Mother, Mary Mother,
Cold bridal cheer, between Hell and Heaven!)

"Three days and nights he has lain abed,
                    Sister Helen,
And he prays in torment to be dead."
"The thing may chance, if he have prayed,
                    Little brother!"
                    (O Mother, Mary Mother,
If he have prayed, between Hell and Heaven!)

"But he has not ceased to cry to-day,
                    Sister Helen,
That you should take your curse away."
"*My* prayer was heard,—he need but pray,
                    Little brother!"
                    (O Mother, Mary Mother,
Shall God not hear, between Hell and Heaven?)

"But he says, till you take back your ban,
                    Sister Helen,
His soul would pass, yet never can."
"Nay then, shall I slay a living man,
                    Little brother?"
                    (O Mother, Mary Mother,
A living soul, between Hell and Heaven!)

"But he calls for ever on your name,
                    Sister Helen,
And says that he melts before a flame."
"My heart for his pleasure fared the same,
                    Little brother."
                    (O Mother, Mary Mother,
Fire at the heart, between Hell and Heaven!)

"Here's Keith of Westholm riding fast,
                    Sister Helen,
For I know the white plume on the blast."
"The hour, the sweet hour I forecast,
                    Little brother!"
                    (O Mother, Mary Mother,
Is the hour sweet, between Hell and Heaven?)

"He stops to speak, and he stills his horse,
                    Sister Helen;
But his words are drowned in the wind's course."
"Nay hear, nay hear, you must hear perforce,
                    Little brother!"
                    (O Mother, Mary Mother,
What word now heard, between Hell and Heaven?)

"Oh he says that Keith of Ewern's cry,
                    Sister Helen,
Is ever to see you ere he die."
"In all that his soul sees, there am I,
                    Little brother!"
                    (O Mother, Mary Mother,
The soul's one sight, between Hell and Heaven!)

"He sends a ring and a broken coin,
                    Sister Helen,
And bids you mind the banks of Boyne."
"What else he broke will he ever join,
                    Little brother?"
                    (O Mother, Mary Mother,
No, never joined, between Hell and Heaven!)

"He yields you these and craves full fain,
                    Sister Helen,
You pardon him in his mortal pain."
"What else he took will he give again,
                    Little brother?"
                    (O Mother, Mary Mother,
Not twice to give, between Hell and Heaven!)

"He calls your name in an agony,
                    Sister Helen,
That even dead Love must weep to see."
"Hate, born of Love, is blind as he,
                    Little brother?"
                    (O Mother, Mary Mother,
Love turned to hate, between Hell and Heaven!)

"Oh it's Keith of Keith now that rides fast,
                    Sister Helen,

For I know the white hair on the blast."
"The short short hour will soon be past,
     Little brother!"
     (O Mother, Mary Mother,
Will soon be past, between Hell and Heaven!)

"He looks at me and he tries to speak,
     Sister Helen,
But oh! his voice is sad and weak!"
"What here should the mighty Baron seek,
     Little brother?"
     (O Mother, Mary Mother,
Is this the end, between Hell and Heaven?)

"Oh his son still cries, if you forgive,
     Sister Helen,
The body dies but the soul shall live."
"Fire shall forgive me as I forgive,
     Little brother!"
     (O Mother, Mary Mother,
As she forgives, between Hell and Heaven!)

"Oh he prays you, as his heart would rive,
     Sister Helen,
To save his dear son's soul alive."
"Fire cannot slay it, it shall thrive,
     Little brother!"
     (O Mother, Mary Mother,
Alas, alas, between Hell and Heaven!)

"He cries to you, kneeling in the road,
     Sister Helen,
To go with him for the love of God!"
"The way is long to his son's abode,
     Little brother."
     (O Mother, Mary Mother,
The way is long, between Hell and Heaven!)

"A lady's here, by a dark steed brought,
     Sister Helen,
So darkly clad, I saw her not."
"See her now or never see aught,
     Little brother!"

(O Mother, Mary Mother,
What more to see, between Hell and Heaven?)

"Her hood falls back, and the moon shines fair,
                    Sister Helen,
On the Lady of Ewern's golden hair."
"Blest hour of my power and her despair,
                    Little brother!"
                    (O Mother, Mary Mother,
Hour blest and bann'd, between Hell and Heaven!)

"Pale, pale her cheeks, that in pride did glow,
                    Sister Helen,
'Neath the bridal-wreath three days ago."
"One morn for pride and three days for woe,
                    Little brother!"
                    (O Mother, Mary Mother,
Three days, three nights, between Hell and Heaven!)

"Her clasped hands stretch from her bending head,
                    Sister Helen;
With the loud wind's wail her sobs are wed."
"What wedding-strains hath her bridal-bed,
                    Little brother?"
                    (O Mother, Mary Mother,
What strain but death's, between Hell and Heaven!)

"She may not speak, she sinks in a swoon,
                    Sister Helen,—
She lifts her lips and gasps on the moon."
"Oh! might I but hear her soul's blithe tune,
                    Little brother!"
                    (O Mother, Mary Mother,
Her woe's dumb cry, between Hell and Heaven!)

"They've caught her to Westholm's saddle-bow,
                    Sister Helen,
And her moonlit hair gleams white in its flow."
"Let it turn whiter than winter snow,
                    Little brother!"

(O Mother, Mary Mother,
Woe-withered gold, between Hell and Heaven!)

"O Sister Helen, you heard the bell,
                    Sister Helen!
More loud than the vesper-chime it fell."
"No vesper-chime, but a dying knell,
                    Little brother!"
          (O Mother, Mary Mother,
His dying knell, between Hell and Heaven!)

"Alas! but I fear the heavy sound,
                    Sister Helen;
Is it in the sky or in the ground?"
"Say, have they turned their horses round,
                    Little brother?"
          (O Mother, Mary Mother,
What would she more, between Hell and Heaven?)

"They have raised the old man from his knee,
                    Sister Helen,
And they ride in silence hastily."
"More fast the naked soul doth flee,
                    Little brother!"
          (O Mother, Mary Mother,
The naked soul, between Hell and Heaven!)

"Flank to flank are the three steeds gone,
                    Sister Helen,
But the lady's dark steed goes alone."
"And lonely her bridegroom's soul hath flown,
                    Little brother."
          (O Mother, Mary Mother,
The lonely ghost, between Hell and Heaven!)

"Oh the wind is sad in the iron chill,
                    Sister Helen,
And weary sad they look by the hill."
"But he and I are sadder still,
                    Little brother!"

(O Mother, Mary Mother,
Most sad of all, between Hell and Heaven!)

"See, see, the wax has dropped from its place,
                    Sister Helen,
And the flames are winning up apace!"
"Yet here they burn but for a space,
                    Little brother!"
            (O Mother, Mary Mother,
Here for a space, between Hell and Heaven!)

"Ah! what white thing at the door has cross'd,
                    Sister Helen?
Ah! what is this that sighs in the frost?"
"A soul that's lost as mine is lost,
                    Little brother!"
            (O Mother, Mary Mother,
Lost, lost, all lost, between Hell and Heaven!)

The Woodspurge

The wind flapped loose, the wind was still,
Shaken out dead from tree and hill:
I had walked on at the wind's will,—
I sat now, for the wind was still.

Between my knees my forehead was,—
My lips, drawn in, said not Alas!
My hair was over in the grass,
My naked ears heard the day pass.

My eyes, wide open, had the run
Of some ten weeds to fix upon;
Among those few, out of the sun,
The woodspurge flowered, three cups in one.

From perfect grief there need not be
Wisdom or even memory:
One thing then learnt remains to me,—
The woodspurge has a cup of three.

Even So

So it is, my dear.
All such things touch secret strings
    For heavy hearts to hear.
    So it is, my dear.

    Very like indeed:
Sea and sky, afar, on high,
    Sand and strewn seaweed, —
    Very like indeed.

    But the sea stands spread
As one wall with the flat skies,
Where the lean black craft like flies
    Seem well-nigh stagnated,
    Soon to drop off dead.

    Seemed it so to us
When I was thine and thou wast mine,
    And all these things were thus,
    But all our world in us?

    Could we be so now?
Not if all beneath heaven's pall
    Lay dead but I and thou,
    Could we be so now!

The Song of the Bower

Say, is it day, is it dusk in thy bower,
    Thou whom I long for, who longest for me?
Oh! be it light, be it night, 'tis Love's hour,
    Love's that is fettered as Love's that is free.
Free Love has leaped to that innermost chamber,
    Oh! the last time, and the hundred before:
Fettered Love, motionless, can but remember,
    Yet something that sighs from him passes the door.

Nay, but my heart when it flies to thy bower,
    What does it find there that knows it again?
There it must droop like a shower-beaten flower,

Red at the rent core and dark with the rain.
Ah! yet what shelter is still shed above it,—
    What waters still image its leaves torn apart?
Thy soul is the shade that clings round it to love it,
    And tears are its mirror deep down in thy heart.

What were my prize, could I enter thy bower,
    This day, to-morrow, at eve or at morn?
Large lovely arms and a neck like a tower,
    Bosom then heaving that now lies forlorn.
Kindled with love-breath, (the sun's kiss is colder!)
    Thy sweetness all near me, so distant to-day;
My hand round thy neck and thy hand on my
        shoulder
    My mouth to thy mouth as the world melts away.

What is it keeps me afar from thy bower,—
    My spirit, my body, so fain to be there?
Waters engulfing or fires that devour?—
    Earth heaped against me or death in the air?
Nay, but in day-dreams, for terror, for pity,
    The trees wave their heads with an omen to tell;
Nay, but in night-dreams, throughout the dark city,
    The hours, clashed together, lose count in the bell.

Shall I not one day remember thy bower,
    One day when all days are one day to me?—
Thinking, "I stirred not, and yet had the power!"—
    Yearning, "Ah God, if again it might be!"
Peace, peace! such a small lamp illumes, on this
        highway,
    So dimly so few steps in front of my feet,—
Yet shows me that her way is parted from my
        way. . . .
    Out of sight, beyond light, at what goal may we
        meet?

First Love Remembered

Peace in her chamber, wheresoe'er
    It be, a holy place:
The thought still brings my soul such grace
    As morning meadows wear.

Whether it still be small and light,
    A maid's who dreams alone,
As from her orchard-gate the moon
    Its ceiling showed at night:

Or whether, in a shadow dense
    As nuptial hymns invoke,
Innocent maidenhood awoke
    To married innocence:

There still the thanks unheard await
    The unconscious gift bequeathed:
For there my soul this hour has breathed
    An air inviolate.

An Old Song Ended

*"How should I your true love know
    From another one?"*
*"By his cockle-hat and staff
    And his sandal-shoon."*

"And what signs have told you now
    That he hastens home?"
"Lo! the spring is nearly gone,
    He is nearly come."

"For a token is there nought,
    Say, that he should bring?"
"He will bear a ring I gave
    And another ring."

"How may I, when he shall ask,
    Tell him who lies there?"
"Nay, but leave my face unveiled
    And unbound my hair."

"Can you say to me some word
    I shall say to him?"
"Say I'm looking in his eyes
    Though my eyes are dim."

Eden Bower

It was Lilith the wife of Adam:
          (*Sing Eden Bower!*)
Not a drop of her blood was human,
But she was made like a soft sweet woman.

Lilith stood on the skirts of Eden;
          (*Alas the hour!*)
She was the first that thence was driven;
With her was hell and with Eve was heaven.

In the ear of the Snake said Lilith:—
          (*Sing Eden Bower!*)
"To thee I come when the rest is over;
A snake was I when thou wast my lover.

"I was the fairest snake in Eden:
          (*Alas the hour!*)
By the earth's will, new form and feature
Made me a wife for the earth's new creature.

"Take me thou as I come from Adam:
          (*Sing Eden Bower!*)
Once again shall my love subdue thee;
The past is past and I am come to thee.

"O but Adam was thrall to Lilith!
          (*Alas the hour!*)
All the threads of my hair are golden,
And there in a net his heart was holden.

"O and Lilith was queen of Adam!
          (*Sing Eden Bower!*)
All the day and the night together
My breath could shake his soul like a feather.

"What great joys had Adam and Lilith!—
          (*Alas the hour!*)
Sweet close rings of the serpent's twining,
As heart in heart lay sighing and pining.

"What bright babes had Lilith and Adam!—
   (Sing Eden Bower!)
Shapes that coiled in the woods and waters,
Glittering sons and radiant daughters.

"O thou God, the Lord God of Eden!
   (Alas the hour!)
Say, was this fair body for no man,
That of Adam's flesh thou mak'st him a woman?

"O thou Snake, the King-snake of Eden!
   (Sing Eden Bower!)
God's strong will our necks are under,
But thou and I may cleave it in sunder.

"Help, sweet Snake, sweet lover of Lilith!
   (Alas the hour!)
And let God learn how I loved and hated
Man in the image of God created.

"Help me once against Eve and Adam!
   (Sing Eden Bower!)
Help me once for this one endeavour,
And then my love shall be thine for ever!

"Strong is God, the fell foe of Lilith:
   (Alas the hour!)
Nought in heaven or earth may affright Him;
But join thou with me and we will smite Him.

"Strong is God, the great God of Eden:
   (Sing Eden Bower!)
Over all He made He hath power;
But lend me thou thy shape for an hour!

"Lend thy shape for the love of Lilith!
   (Alas the hour!)
Look, my mouth and my cheek are ruddy,
And thou art cold, and fire is my body.

"Lend thy shape for the hate of Adam!
   (Sing Eden Bower!)

That he may wail my joy that forsook him,
And curse the day when the bride-sleep took him.

"Lend thy shape for the shame of Eden!
                    (Alas the hour!)
Is not the foe-God weak as the foeman
When love grows hate in the heart of a woman?

"Wouldst thou know the heart's hope of Lilith?
                    (Sing Eden Bower!)
Then bring thou close thine head till it glisten
Along my breast, and lip me and listen.

"Am I sweet, O sweet Snake of Eden?
                    (Alas the hour!)
Then ope thine ear to my warm mouth's cooing
And learn what deed remains for our doing.

"Thou didst hear when God said to Adam:—
                    (Sing Eden Bower!)
'Of all this wealth I have made thee warden;
Thou'rt free to eat of the trees of the garden:

"'Only of one tree eat not in Eden;
                    (Alas the hour!)
All save one I give to thy freewill,—
The Tree of the Knowledge of Good and Evil.'

"O my love, come nearer to Lilith!
                    (Sing Eden Bower!)
In thy sweet folds bind me and bend me,
And let me feel the shape thou shalt lend me!

"In thy shape I'll go back to Eden:
                    (Alas the hour!)
In these coils that Tree will I grapple,
And stretch this crowned head forth by the apple.

"Lo, Eve bends to the breath of Lilith!
                    (Sing Eden Bower!)
O how then shall my heart desire
All her blood as food to its fire!

"Lo, Eve bends to the words of Lilith!—
            (Alas the hour!)
'Nay, this Tree's fruit,—why should ye hate it,
Or Death be born the day that ye ate it?'

"'Nay, but on that great day in Eden,
            (Sing Eden Bower!)
By the help that in this wise Tree is,
God knows well ye shall be as He is.'

"Then Eve shall eat and give unto Adam;
            (Alas the hour!)
And then they both shall know they are naked,
And their hearts ache as my heart hath achèd.

"Ay, let them hide 'mid the trees of Eden,
            (Sing Eden Bower!)
As in the cool of the day in the garden
God shall walk without pity or pardon.

"Hear, thou Eve, the man's heart in Adam!
            (Alas the hour!)
Of his brave words hark to the bravest:—
'This the woman gave that thou gavest.'

"Hear Eve speak, yea list to her, Lilith!
            (Sing Eden Bower!)
Feast thine heart with words that shall sate it—
'This the serpent gave and I ate it.'

"O proud Eve, cling close to thine Adam,
            (Alas the hour!)
Driven forth as the beasts of his naming
By the sword that for ever is flaming.

"Know, thy path is known unto Lilith!
            (Sing Eden Bower!)
While the blithe birds sang at thy wedding,
There her tears grew thorns for thy treading.

"O my love, thou Love-snake of Eden!
            (Alas the hour!)

O to-day and the day to come after!
Loose me, love,—give breath to my laughter.

"O bright Snake, the Death-worm of Adam!
                    (*Sing Eden Bower!*)
Wreathe thy neck with my hair's bright tether,
And wear my gold and thy gold together!

"On that day on the skirts of Eden,
                    (*Alas the hour!*)
In thy shape shall I glide back to thee,
And in my shape for an instant view thee.

"But when thou'rt thou and Lilith is Lilith,
                    (*Sing Eden Bower!*)
In what bliss past hearing or seeing
Shall each one drink of the other's being!

"With cries of 'Eve!' and 'Eden!' and 'Adam!'
                    (*Alas the hour!*)
How shall we mingle our love's caresses,
I in thy coils, and thou in my tresses!

"With those names, ye echoes of Eden,
                    (*Sing Eden Bower!*)
Fire shall cry from my heart that burneth,—
'Dust he is and to dust returneth!'

"Yet to-day, thou master of Lilith,—
                    (*Alas the hour!*)
Wrap me round in the form I'll borrow
And let me tell thee of sweet to-morrow.

"In the planted garden eastward in Eden,
                    (*Sing Eden Bower!*)
Where the river goes forth to water the garden,
The springs shall dry and the soil shall harden.

"Yea, where the bride-sleep fell upon Adam,
                    (*Alas the hour!*)
None shall hear when the storm-wind whistles
Through roses choked among thorns and thistles.

"Yea, beside the east-gate of Eden,
                    (Sing Eden Bower!)
Where God joined them and none might sever,
The sword turns this way and that for ever.

"What of Adam cast out of Eden?
                    (Alas the hour!)
Lo! with care like a shadow shaken,
He tills the hard earth whence he was taken.

"What of Eve too, cast out of Eden?
                    (Sing Eden Bower!)
Nay, but she, the bride of God's giving,
Must yet be mother of all men living.

"Lo, God's grace, by the grace of Lilith!
                    (Alas the hour!)
To Eve's womb, from our sweet to-morrow,
God shall greatly multiply sorrow.

"Fold me fast, O God-snake of Eden!
                    (Sing Eden Bower!)
What more prize than love to impel thee?
Grip and lip my limbs as I tell thee!

"Lo! two babes for Eve and for Adam!
                    (Alas the hour!)
Lo! sweet Snake, the travail and treasure,—
Two men-children born for their pleasure!

"The first is Cain and the second Abel:
                    (Sing Eden Bower!)
The soul of one shall be made thy brother,
And thy tongue shall lap the blood of the other."
                    (Alas the hour!)

Antwerp and Bruges

I climbed the stair in Antwerp church,
    What time the circling thews of sound
    At sunset seem to heave it round.

Far up, the carillon did search
The wind, and the birds came to perch
    Far under, where the gables wound.

In Antwerp harbour on the Scheldt
    I stood along, a certain space
    Of night. The mist was near my face;
Deep on, the flow was heard and felt.
The carillon kept pause, and dwelt
    In music through the silent place.

John Memmeling and John van Eyck
    Hold state at Bruges. In sore shame
    I scanned the works that keep their name.
The carillon, which then did strike
Mine ears, was heard of theirs alike:
    It set me closer unto them.

I climbed at Bruges all the flight
    The belfry has of ancient stone.
    For leagues I saw the east wind blown;
The earth was grey, the sky was white.
I stood so near upon the height
    That my flesh felt the carillon.

Dawn on the Night-Journey

Till dawn the wind drove round me. It is past
    And still, and leaves the air to lisp of bird,
    And to the quiet that is almost heard
Of the new-risen day, as yet bound fast
In the first warmth of sunrise. When the last
    Of the sun's hours to-day shall be fulfilled,
    There shall another breath of time be stilled
For me, which now is to my senses cast
As much beyond me as eternity,
    Unknown, kept secret. On the newborn air
    The moth quivers in silence. It is vast,
Yea, even beyond the hills upon the sea,
    The day whose end shall give this hour as sheer
        As chaos to the irrevocable Past.

During Music

O cool unto the sense of pain
    That last night's sleep could not destroy;
    O warm unto the sense of joy,
That dreams its life within the brain.

What though I lean o'er thee to scan
    The written music cramped and stiff;—
    'Tis dark to me, as hieroglyph
On those weird bulks Egyptian.

But as from those, dumb now and strange,
    A glory wanders on the earth,
    Even so thy tones can call a birth
From these, to shake my soul with change.

O swift, as in melodious haste
    Float o'er the keys thy fingers small;
    O soft, as is the rise and fall
Which stirs that shade within thy breast.

Three Shadows

I looked and saw your eyes
    In the shadow of your hair
As a traveller sees the stream
    In the shadow of the wood;
And I said, "My faint heart sighs
    Ah me! to linger there,
To drink deep and to dream
    In that sweet solitude."

I looked and saw your heart
    In the shadow of your eyes,
As a seeker sees the gold
    In the shadow of the stream;
And I said, "Ah me! what art
    Should win the immortal prize,
Whose want must make life cold
    And Heaven a hollow dream?"

I looked and saw your love
　　In the shadow of your heart,
As a diver sees the pearl
　　In the shadow of the sea;
And I murmured, not above
　　My breath, but all apart,—
"Ah! you can love, true girl,
　　And is your love for me?"

The Orchard-Pit

A Fragment

Piled deep below the screening apple-branch
　　They lie with bitter apples in their hands:
And some are only ancient bones that blanch,
And some had ships that last year's wind did launch,
　　And some were yesterday the lords of lands.

In the soft dell, among the apple-trees,
　　High up above the hidden pit she stands,
And there for ever sings, who gave to these,
That lie below, her magic hour of ease,
　　And those her apples holden in their hands.

This in my dreams is shown me; and her hair
　　Crosses my lips and draws my burning breath;
Her song spreads golden wings upon the air,
Life's eyes are gleaming from her forehead fair,
　　And from her breasts the ravishing eyes of Death.

Men say to me that sleep hath many dreams,
　　Yet I knew never but this dream alone:
There, from a dried-up channel, once the stream's,
The glen slopes up; even such in sleep it seems
　　As to my waking sight the place well known.

*

My love I call her, and she loves me well:
　　But I love her as in the maelstrom's cup
The whirled stone loves the leaf inseparable
That clings to it round all the circling swell,
　　And that the same last eddy swallows up.

Selections from

The House of Life: A Sonnet-Sequence

A Sonnet is a moment's monument,—
*   Memorial from the Soul's eternity*
*   To one dead deathless hour. Look that it be,*
Whether for lustral rite or dire portent,
Of its own arduous fullness reverent:
*   Carve it in ivory or in ebony,*
*   As Day or Night may rule; and let Time see*
Its flowering crest impearled and orient.

A Sonnet is a coin: its face reveals
*   The soul,—its converse, to what Power 'tis due:—*
*   Whether for tribute to the august appeals*
*   Of Life, or dower in Love's high retinue,*
It serve; or, 'mid the dark wharf's cavernous breath,
In Charon's palm it pay the toll to Death.

Part I Youth and Change

SONNET I: Love Enthroned

I marked all kindred Powers the heart finds fair:—
   Truth, with awed lips; and Hope, with eyes upcast;
   And Fame, whose loud wings fan the ashen Past
To signal-fires, Oblivion's flight to scare;
And Youth, with still some single golden hair
   Unto his shoulder clinging, since the last
   Embrace wherein two sweet arms held him fast;
And Life, still wreathing flowers for Death to wear.

Love's throne was not with these; but far above
   All passionate wind of welcome and farewell
He sat in breathless bowers they dream not of;
   Though Truth foreknow Love's heart, and Hope
      foretell,
   And Fame be for Love's sake desirable,
And Youth be dear, and Life be sweet to Love.

SONNET II: Bridal Birth

As when desire, long darkling, dawns, and first
  The mother looks upon the newborn child,
  Even so my Lady stood at gaze and smiled
When her soul knew at length the Love it nurs'd.
Born with her life, creature of poignant thirst
  And exquisite hunger, at her heart Love lay
  Quickening in darkness, till a voice that day
Cried on him, and the bonds of birth were burst.

Now, shadowed by his wings, our faces yearn
  Together, as his full-grown feet now range
    The grove, and his warm hands our couch prepare:
Till to his song our bodiless souls in turn
  Be born his children, when Death's nuptial change
    Leaves us for light the halo of his hair.

SONNET III: Love's Testament

O thou who at Love's hour ecstatically
  Unto my heart dost evermore present,
  Clothed with his fire, thy heart his testament;
Whom I have neared and felt thy breath to be
The inmost incense of his sanctuary;
  Who without speech hast owned him, and, intent
  Upon his will, thy life with mine hast blent,
And murmured, "I am thine, thou'rt one with me!"

O what from thee the grace, to me the prize,
  And what to Love the glory,—when the whole
  Of the deep stair thou tread'st to the dim shoal
And weary water of the place of sighs,
And there dost work deliverance, as thine eyes
  Draw up my prisoned spirit to thy soul!

SONNET IV: Lovesight

When do I see thee most, beloved one?
  When in the light the spirits of mine eyes
  Before thy face, their altar, solemnize
The worship of that Love through thee made known?
  Or when in the dusk hours, (we two alone,)

Closed-kissed and eloquent of still replies
　　Thy twilight-hidden glimmering visage lies,
And my soul only sees thy soul its own?

O love, my love! if I no more should see
Thyself, nor on the earth the shadow of thee,
　　Nor image of thine eyes in any spring,—
How then should sound upon Life's darkening slope
The ground-whirl of the perished leaves of Hope,
　　The wind of Death's imperishable wing?

SONNET VI: The Kiss

What smouldering senses in death's sick delay
　　Or seizure of malign vicissitude
　　Can rob this body of honour, or denude
This soul of wedding-raiment worn to-day?
For lo! even now my lady's lips did play
　　With these my lips such consonant interlude
　　As laurelled Orpheus longed for when he wooed
The half-drawn hungering face with that last lay.

I was a child beneath her touch,—a man
　　When breast to breast we clung, even I and she,—
　　A spirit when her spirit looked through me,—
A god when all our life-breath met to fan
Our life-blood, till love's emulous ardours ran,
　　Fire within fire, desire in deity.

SONNET VIa: Nuptial Sleep

At length their long kiss severed, with sweet smart:
　　And as the last slow sudden drops are shed
　　From sparkling eaves when all the storm has fled,
So singly flagged the pulses of each heart.
Their bosoms sundered, with the opening start
　　Of married flowers to either side outspread
　　From the knit stem; yet still their mouths, burnt red,
Fawned on each other where they lay apart.

Sleep sank them lower than the tide of dreams,
　　And their dreams watched them sink, and slid away.
Slowly their souls swarm up again, through gleams

Of watered light and dull drowned waifs of day;
Till from some wonder of new woods and streams
   He woke, and wondered more: for there she lay.

SONNET VII: Supreme Surrender

To all the spirits of Love that wander by
   Along his love-sown harvest-field of sleep
   My lady lies apparent; and the deep
Calls to the deep; and no man sees but I.
The bliss so long afar, at length so nigh,
   Rests there attained. Methinks proud Love must weep
   When Fate's control doth from his harvest reap
The sacred hour for which the years did sigh.

First touched, the hand now warm around my neck
   Taught memory long to mock desire: and lo!
   Across my breast the abandoned hair doth flow,
Where one shorn tress long stirred the longing ache:
And next the heart that trembled for its sake
   Lies the queen-heart in sovereign overthrow.

SONNET X: The Portrait

O Lord of all compassionate control,
   O Love! let this my lady's picture glow
   Under my hand to praise her name, and show
Even of her inner self the perfect whole:
That he who seeks her beauty's furthest goal,
   Beyond the light that the sweet glances throw
   And refluent wave of the sweet smile, may know
The very sky and sea-line of her soul.

Lo! it is done. Above the enthroning throat
   The mouth's mould testifies of voice and kiss,
   The shadowed eyes remember and foresee.
Her face is made her shrine. Let all men note
   That in all years (O Love, thy gift is this!)
     They that would look on her must come to me.

SONNET XIII: Youth's Antiphony

"I love you, sweet: how can you ever learn
    How much I love you?" "You I love even so,
    And so I learn it." "Sweet, you cannot know
How fair you are." "If fair enough to earn
Your love, so much is all my love's concern."
    "My love grows hourly, sweet." "Mine too doth grow,
    Yet love seemed full so many hours ago!"
Thus lovers speak, till kisses claim their turn.

Ah! happy they to whom such words as these
    In youth have served for speech the whole day long,
    Hour after hour, remote from the world's throng,
Work, contest, fame, all life's confederate pleas,—
What while Love breathed in sighs and silences
    Through two blent souls one rapturous undersong.

SONNET XIV: Youth's Spring-Tribute

On this sweet bank your head thrice sweet and dear
    I lay, and spread your hair on either side,
    And see the newborn woodflowers bashful-eyed
Look through the golden tresses here and there.
On these debateable borders of the year
    Spring's foot half falters; scarce she yet may know
    The leafless blackthorn-blossom from the snow;
And through her bowers the wind's way still is clear.

But April's sun strikes down the glades to-day;
    So shut your eyes upturned, and feel my kiss
Creep, as the Spring now thrills through every spray,
    Up your warm throat to your warm lips: for this
    Is even the hour of Love's sworn suitservice,
With whom cold hearts are counted castaway.

SONNET XVI: A Day of Love

Those envied places which do know her well,
    And are so scornful of this lonely place,
    Even now for once are emptied of her grace:

Nowhere but here she is: and while Love's spell
From his predominant presence doth compel
    All alien hours, an outworn populace,
    The hours of Love fill full the echoing space
With sweet confederate music favourable.

Now many memories make solicitous
    The delicate love-lines of her mouth, till, lit
    With quivering fire, the words take wing from it;
As here between our kisses we sit thus
    Speaking of things remembered, and so sit
Speechless while things forgotten call to us.

SONNET XIX: Silent Noon

Your hands lie open in the long fresh grass, —
    The finger-points look through like rosy blooms:
    Your eyes smile peace. The pasture gleams and glooms
'Neath billowing skies that scatter and amass.
All round our nest, far as the eye can pass,
    Are golden kingcup-fields with silver edge
    Where the cow-parsley skirts the hawthorn-hedge.
'Tis visible silence, still as the hour-glass.

Deep in the sun-searched growths the dragon-fly
Hangs like a blue thread loosened from the sky: —
    So this wing'd hour is dropt to us from above.
Oh! clasp we to our hearts, for deathless dower,
This close-companioned inarticulate hour
    When twofold silence was the song of love.

SONNET XX: Gracious Moonlight

Even as the moon grows queenlier in mid-space
    When the sky darkens, and her cloud-rapt car
    Thrills with intenser radiance from afar, —
So lambent, lady, beams thy sovereign grace
When the drear soul desire thee. Of that face
    What shall be said, — which, like a governing star,
    Gathers and garners from all things that are
Their silent penetrative loveliness?

O'er water-daisies and wild waifs of Spring,
    There where the iris rears its gold-crowned sheaf
    With flowering rush and sceptred arrow-leaf,
So have I marked Queen Dian, in bright ring
Of cloud above and wave below, take wing
    And chase night's gloom, as thou the spirit's grief.

SONNET XXII: Heart's Haven

Sometimes she is a child within mine arms,
    Cowering beneath dark wings that love must chase,—
    With still tears showering and averted face,
Inexplicably filled with faint alarms:
And oft from mine own spirit's hurtling harms
    I crave the refuge of her deep embrace,—
    Against all ills the fortified strong place
And sweet reserve of sovereign counter-charms.

And Love, our light at night and shade at noon,
    Lulls us to rest with songs, and turns away
    All shafts of shelterless tumultuous day.
Like the moon's growth, his face gleams through his tune;
And as soft waters warble to the moon,
    Our answering spirits chime one roundelay.

SONNET XXV: Winged Hours

Each hour until we meet is as a bird
    That wings from far his gradual way along
    The rustling covert of my soul,—his song
Still loudlier trilled through leaves more deeply stirr'd:
But at the hour of meeting, a clear word
    Is every note he sings, in Love's own tongue:
    Yet, Love, thou know'st the sweet strain suffers wrong,
Full oft through our contending joys unheard.

What of that hour at last, when for her sake
    No wing may fly to me nor song may flow;
    When, wandering round my life unleaved, I know
The bloodied feathers scattered in the brake,
And think how she, far from me, with like eyes
Sees through the untuneful bough the wingless skies?

SONNET XXVI: Mid-Rapture

Thou lovely and beloved, thou my love;
   Whose kiss seems still the first; whose summoning eyes,
   Even now, as for our love-world's new sunrise,
Shed very dawn; whose voice, attuned above
All modulation of the deep-bowered dove,
   Is like a hand laid softly on the soul;
   Whose hand is like a sweet voice to control
Those worn tired brows it hath the keeping of:—

What word can answer to thy word,—what gaze
   To thine, which now absorbs within its sphere
   My worshiping face, till I am mirrored there
Light-circled in a heaven of deep-drawn rays?
What clasp, what kiss mine inmost heart can prove,
O lovely and beloved, O my love?

SONNET XXXIV: The Dark Glass

Not I myself know all my love for thee:
   How should I reach so far, who cannot weigh
   To-morrow's dower by gage of yesterday?
Shall birth and death, and all dark names that be
As doors and windows bared to some loud sea,
   Lash deaf mine ears and blind my face with spray;
   And shall my sense pierce love,—the last relay
And ultimate outpost of eternity?

Lo! what am I to Love, the lord of all?
   One murmuring shell he gathers from the sand,—
   One little heart-flame sheltered in his hand.
Yet through thine eyes he grants me clearest call
And veriest touch of powers primordial
   That any hour-girt life may understand.

SONNET XXXV: The Lamp's Shrine

Sometimes I fain would find in thee some fault,
   That I might love thee still in spite of it:
   Yet how should our Lord Love curtail one whit

Thy perfect praise whom most he would exalt?
Alas! he can but make my heart's low vault
   Even in men's sight unworthier, being lit
   By thee, who thereby show'st more exquisite
Like fiery chrysoprase in deep basalt.

Yet will I nowise shrink; but at Love's shrine
   Myself within the beams his brow doth dart
   Will set the flashing jewel of thy heart
In that dull chamber where it deigns to shine:
For lo! in honour of thine excellencies
My heart takes pride to show how poor it is.

SONNET XXXVI: Life-in-Love

Not in thy body is thy life at all,
   But in this lady's lips and hands and eyes;
   Through these she yields thee life that vivifies
What else were sorrow's servant and death's thrall.
Look on thyself without her, and recall
   The waste remembrance and forlorn surmise
   That lived but in a dead-drawn breath of sighs
O'er vanished hours and hours eventual.

Even so much life hath the poor tress of hair
   Which, stored apart, is all love hath to show
   For heart-beats and for fire-heats long ago;
Even so much life endures unknown, even where,
'Mid change the changeless night environeth,
Lies all that golden hair undimmed in death.

SONNET XL: Severed Selves

Two separate divided silences,
   Which, brought together, would find loving voice;
   Two glances which together would rejoice
In love, now lost like stars beyond dark trees;
Two hands apart whose touch alone gives ease;
   Two bosoms which, heart-shrined with mutual flame,
   Would, meeting in one clasp, be made the same;
Two souls, the shores wave-mocked of sundering seas: —

Such are we now. Ah! may our hope forecast
    Indeed one hour again, when on this stream
    Of darkened love once more the light shall gleam?—
An hour how slow to come, how quickly past,—
Which blooms and fades, and only leaves at last,
    Faint as shed flowers, the attenuated dream.

SONNET XLIII: Love and Hope

Bless love and hope. Full many a withered year
    Whirled past us, eddying to its chill doomsday;
    And clasped together where the blown leaves lay
We long have knelt and wept full many a tear.
Yet lo! one hour at last, the Spring's compeer,
    Flutes softly to us from some green byeway:
    Those years, those tears are dead, but only they:—
Bless love and hope, true soul; for we are here.

Cling heart to heart; nor of this hour demand
    Whether in very truth, when we are dead,
    Our hearts shall wake to know Love's golden head
Sole sunshine of the imperishable land;
Or but discern, through night's unfeatured scope,
Scorn-fired at length the illusive eyes of Hope.

SONNET XLIV: Cloud and Wind

Love, should I fear death most for you or me?
    Yet if you die, can I not follow you,
    Forcing the straits of change? Alas! but who
Shall wrest a bond from night's inveteracy,
Ere yet my hazardous soul put forth, to be
    Her warrant against all her haste might rue?—
    Ah! in your eyes so reached what dumb adieu,
What unsunned gyres of waste eternity?

And if I die the first, shall death be then
    A lampless watchtower whence I see you weep?—
    Or (woe is me!) a bed wherein my sleep
Ne'er notes (as death's dear cup at last you drain)
The hour when you too learn that all is vain
    And that Hope sows what Love shall never reap?

SONNET XLVII: Broken Music

The mother will not turn, who thinks she hears
    Her nursling's speech first grow articulate;
    But breathless with averted eyes elate
She sits, with open lips and open ears,
That it may call her twice. 'Mid doubts and fears
    Thus oft my soul has hearkened; till the song,
    A central moan for days, at length found tongue,
And the sweet music welled and the sweet tears.

But now, whatever while the soul is fain
    To list that wonted murmur, as it were
The speech-bound sea-shell's low importunate strain,—
    No breath of song, thy voice alone is there,
O bitterly beloved! and all her gain
    Is but the pang of unpermitted prayer.

SONNET XLVIII: Death-in-Love

There came an image in Life's retinue
    That had Love's wings and bore his gonfalon:
    Fair was the web, and nobly wrought thereon,
O soul-sequestered face, thy form and hue!
Bewildering sounds, such as Spring wakens to,
    Shook in its folds; and through my heart its power
    Sped trackless as the immemorable hour
When birth's dark portal groaned and all was new.

But a veiled woman followed, and she caught
    The banner round its staff, to furl and cling,
    Then plucked a feather from the bearer's wing,
And held it to his lips that stirred it not,
And said to me, "Behold, there is no breath:
I and this Love are one, and I am Death."

SONNETS XLIX, L, LI, LII: Willowwood

I
I sat with Love upon a woodside well,
    Leaning across the water, I and he;
    Nor ever did he speak nor looked at me,

But touched his lute wherein was audible
The certain secret thing he had to tell:
  Only our mirrored eyes met silently
  In the low wave; and that sound came to be
The passionate voice I knew; and my tears fell.

And at their fall, his eyes beneath grew hers;
And with his foot and with his wing-feathers
  He swept the spring that watered my heart's drouth.
Then the dark ripples spread to waving hair,
And as I stooped, her own lips rising there
  Bubbled with brimming kisses at my mouth.

II
And now Love sang: but his was such a song
  So meshed with half-remembrance hard to free,
  As souls disused in death's sterility
May sing when the new birthday tarries long.
And I was made aware of a dumb throng
  That stood aloof, one form by ever tree,
  All mournful forms, for each was I or she,
The shades of those our days that had no tongue.

They looked on us, and knew us and were known;
  While fast together, alive from the abyss,
  Clung the soul-wrung implacable close kiss;
And pity of self through all made broken moan
Which said, "For once, for once, for once alone!"
  And still Love sang, and what he sang was this:—

III
"O ye, all ye that walk in Willowwood,
  That walk with hollow faces burning white;
What fathom-depth of soul-struck widowhood,
  What long, what longer hours, one lifelong night,
Ere ye again, who so in vain have wooed
  Your last hope lost, who so in vain invite
Your lips to that their unforgotten food,
  Ere ye, ere ye again shall see the light!

Alas! the bitter banks in Willowwood,
    With tear-spurge wan, with blood-wort burning red:
Alas! if ever such a pillow could
    Steep deep the soul in sleep till she were dead,—
Better all life forget her than this thing,
That Willowwood should hold her wandering!"

IV
So sang he: and as meeting rose and rose
    Together cling through the wind's wellaway
    Nor change at once, yet near the end of day
The leaves drop loosened where the heart-stain glows,—
So when the song died did the kiss unclose;
    And her face fell back drowned, and was as grey
    As its grey eyes; and if it ever may
Meet mine again I know not if Love knows.

Only I know that I leaned low and drank
A long draught from the water where she sank,
    Her breath and all her tears and all her soul:
And as I leaned, I know I felt Love's face
Pressed on my neck with moan of pity and grace,
    Till both our heads were in his aureole.

SONNET LIII: Without Her

What of her glass without her? The blank grey
    There where the pool is blind of the moon's face.
    Her dress without her? The tossed empty space
Of cloud-rack whence the moon has passed away.
Her paths without her? Day's appointed sway
    Usurped by desolate night. Her pillowed place
    Without her? Tears, ah me! for love's good grace,
And cold forgetfulness of night or day.

What of the heart without her? Nay, poor heart,
    Of thee what word remains ere speech be still?
    A wayfarer by barren ways and chill,
Steep ways and weary, without her thou art,
Where the long cloud, the long wood's counterpart,
    Sheds doubled darkness up the labouring hill.

SONNETS LVI, LVII, LVIII: True Woman

I   Herself
To be a sweetness more desired than Spring;
   A bodily beauty more acceptable
   Than the wild rose-tree's arch that crowns the fell;
To be an essence more environing
Than wine's drained juice; a music ravishing
   More than the passionate pulse of Philomel;—
   To be all this 'neath one soft bosom's swell
That is the flower of life:—how strange a thing!

How strange a thing to be what Man can know
   But as a sacred secret! Heaven's own screen
Hides her soul's purest depth and loveliest glow;
   Closely withheld, as all things most unseen,—
   The wave-bowered pearl,—the heart-shaped seal of green
That flecks the snowdrop underneath the snow.

II   Her Love
She loves him; for her infinite soul is Love,
   And he her lodestar. Passion in her is
   A glass facing his fire, where the bright bliss
Is mirrored, and the heat returned. Yet move
That glass, a stranger's amorous flame to prove,
   And it shall turn, by instant contraries,
   Ice to the moon; while her pure fire to his
For whom it burns, clings close i' the heart's alcove.

Lo! they are one. With wifely breast to breast
   And circling arms, she welcomes all command
   Of love,—her soul to answering ardours fann'd:
Yet as morn springs or twilight sinks to rest,
Ah! who shall say she deems not loveliest
   The hour of sisterly sweet hand-in-hand?

III   Her Heaven
If to grow old in Heaven is to grow young,
   (As the Seer saw and said,) then blest were he
   With youth for evermore, whose heaven should be
True Woman, she whom these weak notes have sung.
Here and hereafter,—choir-strains of her tongue,—

Sky-spaces of her eyes,—sweet signs that flee
   About her soul's immediate sanctuary,—
Were Paradise all uttermost worlds among.
The sunrise blooms and withers on the hill
   Like any hillflower; and the noblest troth
   Dies here to dust. Yet shall Heaven's promise clothe
Even yet those lovers who have cherished still
This test for love:—in every kiss sealed fast
To feel the first kiss and forebode the last.

SONNET LIX: Love's Last Gift

Love to his singer held a glistening leaf,
   And said: "The rose-tree and the apple-tree
   Have fruits to vaunt or flowers to lure the bee;
And golden shafts are in the feathered sheaf
Of the great harvest-marshal, the year's chief,
   Victorious Summer; aye, and 'neath warm sea
   Strange secret grasses lurk inviolably
Between the filtering channels of sunk reef.

All are my blooms; and all sweet blooms of love
   To thee I gave while Spring and Summer sang;
   But Autumn stops to listen, with some pang
From those worse things the wind is moaning of.
Only this laurel dreads no winter days:
Take my last gift; thy heart hath sung my praise.

Part II Change and Fate
SONNET LX: Transfigured Life

As growth of form or momentary glance
   In a child's features will recall to mind
   The father's with the mother's face combin'd,—
Sweet interchange that memories still enhance:
And yet, as childhood's years and youth's advance,
   The gradual mouldings leave one stamp behind,
   Till in the blended likeness now we find
A separate man's or woman's countenance:—

So in the Song, the singer's Joy and Pain,
　　Its very parents, evermore expand
To bid the passion's fullgrown birth remain,
　　By Art's transfiguring essence subtly spann'd;
　　And from that song-cloud shaped as a man's hand
There comes the sound as of abundant rain.

SONNET LXVI: The Heart of the Night

From child to youth; from youth to arduous man;
　　From lethargy to fever of the heart;
　　　From faithful life to dream-dowered days apart;
From trust to doubt; from doubt to brink of ban;—
Thus much of change in one swift cycle ran
　　Till now. Alas, the soul!—how soon must she
　　Accept her primal immortality,—
The flesh resume its dust whence it began?

O Lord of work and peace! O Lord of life!
　　O Lord, the awful Lord of will! though late,
　　　Even yet renew this soul with duteous breath:
That when the peace is garnered in from strife,
　　The work retrieved, the will regenerate,
　　　This soul may see thy face, O Lord of death!

SONNET LXIX: Autumn Idleness

This sunlight shames November where he grieves
　　In dead red leaves, and will not let him shun
　　　The day, though bough with bough be over-run.
But with a blessing every glade receives
High salutation; while from hillock-eaves
　　The deer gaze calling, dappled white and dun,
　　As if, being foresters of old, the sun
Had marked them with the shade of forest-leaves.

Here dawn to-day unveiled her magic glass;
　　Here noon now gives the thirst and takes the dew;
Till eve bring rest when other good things pass.
　　And here the lost hours the lost hours renew
While I still lead my shadow o'er the grass,
　　Nor know, for longing, that which I should do.

SONNET LXX: The Hill Summit

This feast-day of the sun, his altar there
   In the broad west has blazed for vesper-song;
   And I have loitered in the vale too long
And gaze now a belated worshiper.
Yet may I not forget that I was 'ware,
   So journeying, of his face at intervals
   Transfigured where the fringed horizon falls,—
A fiery bush with coruscating hair.

And now that I have climbed and won this height,
   I must tread downward through the sloping shade
And travel the bewildered tracks till night.
   Yet for this hour I still may here be stayed
   And see the gold air and the silver fade
And the last bird fly into the last light.

SONNET LXXVII: Soul's Beauty

Under the arch of Life, where love and death,
   Terror and mystery, guard her shrine, I saw
   Beauty enthroned; and though her gaze struck awe,
I drew it in as simply as my breath.
Hers are the eyes which, over and beneath,
   The sky and sea bend on thee,—which can draw,
   By sea or sky or woman, to one law,
The allotted bondman of her palm and wreath.

This is that Lady Beauty, in whose praise
   Thy voice and hand shake still,—long known to thee
     By flying hair and fluttering hem,—the beat
     Following her daily of thy heart and feet,
   How passionately and irretrievably,
In what fond flight, how many ways and days!

SONNET LXXVIII: Body's Beauty

Of Adam's first wife, Lilith, it is told
   (The witch he loved before the gift of Eve,)
   That, ere the snake's, her sweet tongue could deceive,
And her enchanted hair was the first gold.

And still she sits, young while the earth is old,
   And, subtly of herself contemplative,
   Draws men to watch the bright web she can weave,
Till heart and body and life are in its hold.

The rose and poppy are her flowers; for where
   Is he not found, O Lilith, whom shed scent
And soft-shed kisses and soft sleep shall snare?
   Lo! as that youth's eyes burned at thine, so went
   Thy spell through him, and left his straight neck bent
And round his heart one strangling golden hair.

SONNET LXXX: From Dawn to Noon

As the child knows not if his mother's face
   Be fair; nor of his elders yet can deem
   What each most is; but as of hill or stream
At dawn, all glimmering life surrounds his place:
Who yet, tow'rd noon of his half-weary race,
   Pausing awhile beneath the high sun-beam
   And gazing steadily back,—as through a dream,
In things long past new features now can trace:—

Even so the thought that is at length fullgrown
   Turns back to note the sun-smit paths, all grey
And marvellous once, where first it walked alone;
   And haply doubts, amid the unblenching day,
   Which most or least impelled its onward way,—
Those unknown things or these things overknown.

SONNET LXXXI: Memorial Thresholds

What place so strange,—though unrevealèd snow
   With unimaginable fires arise
   At the earth's end,—what passion of surprise
Like frost-bound fire-girt scenes of long ago?
Lo! this is none but I this hour; and lo!
   This is the very place which to mine eyes
   Those mortal hours in vain immortalize,
'Mid hurrying crowds, with what alone I know.

City, of thine a single simple door,
   By some new Power reduplicate, must be
   Even yet my life-porch in eternity,
Even with one presence filled, as once of yore:
Or mocking winds whirl round a chaff-strown floor
   Thee and thy years and these my words and me.

SONNET LXXXV: Vain Virtues

What is the sorriest thing that enters Hell?
   None of the sins,—but this and that fair deed
   Which a soul's sin at length could supersede.
These yet are virgins, whom death's timely knell
Might once have sainted; whom the fiends compel
   Together now, in snake-bound shuddering sheaves
   Of anguish, while the pit's pollution leaves
Their refuse maidenhood abominable.

Night sucks them down, the tribute of the pit,
   Whose names, half entered in the book of Life,
     Were God's desire at noon. And as their hair
And eyes sink last, the Torturer deigns no whit
   To gaze, but, yearning, waits his destined wife,
     The Sin still blithe on earth that sent them there.

SONNET LXXXVI: Lost Days

The lost days of my life until to-day,
   What were they, could I see them on the street
   Lie as they fell? Would they be ears of wheat
Sown once for food but trodden into clay?
Or golden coins squandered and still to pay?
   Or drops of blood dabbling the guilty feet?
   Or such spilt water as in dreams must cheat
The undying throats of Hell, athirst alway?

I do not see them here; but after death
   God knows I know the faces I shall see,
Each one a murdered self, with low last breath.
   "I am thyself,—what hast thou done to me?"
"And I—and I—thyself," (lo! each one saith,)
   "And thou thyself to all eternity!"

SONNET XCI: Lost on Both Sides

As when two men have loved a woman well,
    Each hating each, through Love's and Death's deceit;
    Since not for either this stark marriage-sheet
And the long pauses of this wedding-bell;
    Yet o'er her grave the night and day dispel
    At last their feud forlorn, with cold and heat;
    Nor other than dear friends to death may fleet
The two lives left that most of her can tell:—

So separate hopes, which in a soul had wooed
    The one same Peace, strove with each other long,
    And Peace before their faces perished since:
So through that soul, in restless brotherhood,
    They roam together now, and wind among
    Its bye-streets, knocking at the dusty inns.

SONNET XCVII: A Superscription

Look in my face; my name is Might-have-been;
    I am also called No-more, Too-late, Farewell;
    Unto thine ear I hold the dead-sea shell
Cast up thy Life's foam-fretted feet between;
Unto thine eyes the glass where that is seen
    Which had Life's form and Love's, but by my spell
    Is now a shaken shadow intolerable,
Of ultimate things unuttered the frail screen.

Mark me, how still I am! But should there dart
    One moment through thy soul the soft surprise
    Of that winged Peace which lulls the breath of sighs,—
Then shalt thou see me smile, and turn apart
Thy visage to mine ambush at thy heart
    Sleepless with cold commemorative eyes.

SONNET XCVIII: He and I

Whence came his feet into my field, and why?
    How is it that he sees it all so drear?
    How do I see his seeing, and how hear
The name his bitter silence knows it by?

This was the little fold of separate sky
   Whose pasturing clouds in the soul's atmosphere
   Drew living light from one continual year:
How should he find it lifeless? He, or I?

Lo! this new Self now wanders round my field,
   With plaints for every flower, and for each tree
   A moan, the sighing wind's auxiliary:
And o'er sweet waters of my life, that yield
Unto his lips no draught but tears unseal'd,
   Even in my place he weeps. Even I, not he.

SONNETS XCIX, C: Newborn Death

I

To-day Death seems to me an infant child
   Which her worn mother Life upon my knee
   Has set to grow my friend and play with me;
If haply so my heart might be beguil'd
To find no terrors in a face so mild,—
   If haply so my weary heart might be
   Unto the newborn milky eyes of thee,
O Death, before resentment reconcil'd.

How long, O Death? And shall thy feet depart
   Still a young child's with mine, or wilt thou stand
Fullgrown the helpful daughter of my heart,
   What time with thee indeed I reach the strand
Of the pale wave which knows thee what thou art,
   And drink it in the hollow of thy hand?

II

And thou, O Life, the lady of all bliss,
   With whom, when our first heart beat full and fast,
   I wandered till the haunts of men were pass'd,
And in fair places found all bowers amiss
Till only woods and waves might hear our kiss,
   While to the winds all thought of Death we cast:—
   Ah, Life! and must I have from thee at last
No smile to greet me and no babe but this?

Lo! Love, the child once ours; and Song, whose hair
  Blew like a flame and blossomed like a wreath;
And Art, whose eyes were worlds by God found fair:
  These o'er the book of Nature mixed their breath
With neck-twined arms, as oft we watched them there;
  And did these die that thou mightst bear me Death?

SONNET CI: The One Hope

When vain desire at last and vain regret
  Go hand in hand to death, and all is vain,
  What shall assuage the unforgotten pain
And teach the unforgetful to forget?
Shall Peace be still a sunk stream long unmet,—
  Or may the soul at once in a green plain
  Stoop through the spray of some sweet life-fountain
And cull the dew-drenched flowering amulet?

Ah! when the wan soul in that golden air
  Between the scriptured petals softly blown
  Peers breathless for the gift of grace unknown,—
Ah! let none other alien spell soe'er
But only the one Hope's one name be there,
  Not less nor more, but even that world alone.

CHRISTINA ROSSETTI
(1830–1894)

Sister of Dante Gabriel Rossetti, Christina Rossetti belonged to the inner circle of the Brotherhood, and contributed verse to *The Germ*, the official publication of the group. Indeed, her *Goblin Market and Other Poems* (1862) was the first great literary success the Brotherhood enjoyed. In the range and quality of her output she ranks among the most important nineteenth-century English poets. Elegiac and haunting, her poetry often involves poignant musings on the brevity of life, the transience of beauty in the natural world, and devotional verse. Her exquisitely crafted religious poetry is perhaps closest in spirit to the original aims and piety of the Pre-Raphaelites.

Dream Land

Where sunless rivers weep
Their waves into the deep,
She sleeps a charmèd sleep:
    Awake her not.
Led by a single star,
She came from very far
To seek where shadows are
    Her pleasant lot.

She left the rosy morn,
She left the fields of corn,
For twilight cold and lorn
    And water springs.
Through sleep, as through a veil,

She sees the sky look pale,
And hears the nightingale
    That sadly sings.

Rest, rest, a perfect rest
Shed over brow and breast;
Her face is toward the west,
    The purple land.
She cannot see the grain
Ripening on hill and plain;
She cannot feel the rain
    Upon her hand.

Rest, rest, for evermore
Upon a mossy shore;
Rest, rest at the heart's core
    Till time shall cease:
Sleep that no pain shall wake,
Night that no morn shall break
Till joy shall overtake
    Her perfect peace.

At Home

When I was dead, my spirit turned
    To seek the much-frequented house:
I passed the door, and saw my friends
    Feasting beneath the green orange boughs;
From hand to hand they pushed the wine,
    They sucked the pulp of plum and peach;
They sang, they jested, and they laughed,
    For each was loved of each.

I listened to their honest chat:
    Said one: "To-morrow we shall be
Plod plod along the featureless sands
    And coasting miles and miles of sea."
Said one: "Before the turn of tide
    We will achieve the eyrie-seat."
Said one: "To-morrow shall be like
    To-day, but much more sweet."

"To-morrow," said they, strong with hope,
   And dwelt upon the pleasant way:
"To-morrow," cried they one and all,
   While no one spoke of yesterday.
Their life stood full at blessed noon;
   I, only I, had passed away:
"To-morrow and to-day," they cried;
   I was of yesterday.

I shivered comfortless, but cast
   No chill across the tablecloth;
I all-forgotten shivered, sad
   To stay and yet to part how loth:
I passed from the familiar room,
   I who from love had passed away,
Like the remembrance of a guest
   That tarrieth but a day.

A Triad

SONNET

Three sang of love together: one with lips
   Crimson, with cheeks and bosom in a glow,
Flushed to the yellow hair and finger-tips;
   And one there sang who soft and smooth as snow
   Bloomed like a tinted hyacinth at a show;
And one was blue with famine after love,
   Who like a harpstring snapped rang harsh and low
The burden of what those were singing of.
One shamed herself in love; one temperately
   Grew gross in soulless love, a sluggish wife;
One famished died for love. Thus two of three
   Took death for love and won him after strife;
One droned in sweetness like a fattened bee:
   All on the threshold, yet all short of life.

Cousin Kate

I was a cottage maiden
   Hardened by sun and air,
Contented with my cottage mates,
   Not mindful I was fair.

Why did a great lord find me out,
    And praise my flaxen hair?
Why did a great lord find me out
    To fill my heart with care?

He lured me to his palace home—
    Woe's me for joy thereof—
To lead a shameless shameful life,
    His plaything and his love.
He wore me like a silken knot,
    He changed me like a glove;
So now I moan, an unclean thing,
    Who might have been a dove.

O Lady Kate, my cousin Kate,
    You grew more fair than I:
He saw you at your father's gate,
    Chose you, and cast me by.
He watched your steps along the lane,
    Your work among the rye;
He lifted you from mean estate
    To sit with him on high.

Because you were so good and pure
    He bound you with his ring:
The neighbours call you good and pure,
    Call me an outcast thing.
Even so I sit and howl in dust,
    You sit in gold and sing:
Now which of us has tenderer heart?
    You had the stronger wing.

O cousin Kate, my love was true,
    Your love was writ in sand:
If he had fooled not me but you,
    If you stood where I stand,
He'd not have won me with his love
    Nor bought me with his land;
I would have spit into his face
    And not have taken his hand.

Yet I've a gift you have not got,
   And seem not like to get:
For all your clothes and wedding-ring
   I've little doubt you fret.
My fair-haired son, my shame, my pride,
   Cling closer, closer yet:
Your father would give lands for one
   To wear his coronet.

Spring

Frost-locked all the winter,
Seeds, and roots, and stones of fruits,
What shall make their sap ascend
That they may put forth shoots?
Tips of tender green,
Leaf, or blade, or sheath;
Telling of the hidden life
That breaks forth underneath,
Life nursed in its grave by Death.

Blows the thaw-wind pleasantly,
Drips the soaking rain,
By fits looks down the waking sun:
Young grass springs on the plain;
Young leaves clothe early hedgerow trees;
Seeds, and roots, and stones of fruits,
Swollen with sap put forth their shoots;
Curled-headed ferns sprout in the lane;
Birds sing and pair again.

There is no time like Spring,
When life's alive in everything,
Before new nestlings sing,
Before cleft swallows speed their journey back
Along the trackless track—
God guides their wing,
He spreads their table that they nothing lack,—
Before the daisy grows a common flower,
Before the sun has power
To scorch the world up in his noontide hour.

There is no time like Spring,
Like Spring that passes by:
There is no life like Spring-life born to die,—
Piercing the sod,
Clothing the uncouth clod,
Hatched in the nest,
Fledged on the windy bough,
Strong on the wing;
There is no time like Spring that passes by,
Now newly born, and now
Hastening to die.

A Birthday

My heart is like a singing bird
    Whose nest is in a watered shoot;
My heart is like an apple-tree
    Whose boughs are bent with thick-set fruit;
My heart is like a rainbow shell
    That paddles in a halcyon sea;
My heart is gladder than all these
    Because my love is come to me.

Raise me a dais of silk and down;
    Hang it with vair and purple dyes;
Carve it in doves, and pomegranates,
    And peacocks with a hundred eyes;
Work it in gold and silver grapes,
    In leaves, and silver fleurs-de-lys;
Because the birthday of my life
    Is come, my love is come to me.

Remember

SONNET

Remember me when I am gone away,
    Gone far away into the silent land;
    When you can no more hold me by the hand,
Nor I half turn to go yet turning stay.
Remember me when no more day by day
    You tell me of our future that you planned:
    Only remember me; you understand
It will be late to counsel then or pray.

Yet if you should forget me for a while
    And afterwards remember, do not grieve:
    For if the darkness and corruption leave
    A vestige of the thoughts that once I had,
Better by far you should forget and smile
    Than that you should remember and be sad.

After Death

SONNET

The curtains were half drawn, the floor was swept
    And strewn with rushes, rosemary and may
    Lay thick upon the bed on which I lay,
Where through the lattice ivy-shadows crept.
He leaned above me, thinking that I slept
    And could not hear him; but I heard him say:
    "Poor child, poor child": and as he turned away
Came a deep silence, and I knew he wept.
He did not touch the shroud, or raise the fold
    That hid my face, or take my hand in his,
        Or ruffle the smooth pillows for my head:
        He did not love me living; but once dead
    He pitied me; and very sweet it is
To know he still is warm though I am cold.

An End

Love, strong as Death, is dead.
Come, let us make his bed
Among the dying flowers:
A green turf at his head;
And a stone at his feet,
Whereon we may sit
In the quiet evening hours.

He was born in the Spring,
And died before the harvesting:
On the last warm summer day
He left us; he would not stay
For Autumn twilight cold and grey.
Sit we by his grave, and sing
He is gone away.

To few chords and sad and low
Sing we so:
Be our eyes fixed on the grass
Shadow-veiled as the years pass
While we think of all that was
In the long ago.

Song

Oh roses for the flush of youth,
    And laurel for the perfect prime;
But pluck an ivy branch for me
    Grown old before my time.

Oh violets for the grave of youth,
    And bay for those dead in their prime;
Give me the withered leaves I chose
    Before in the old time.

A Summer Wish

Live all thy sweet life thro',
    Sweet Rose, dew-sprent,
Drop down thine evening dew
To gather it anew
When day is bright:
    I fancy thou wast meant
Chiefly to give delight.

Sing in the silent sky,
    Glad soaring bird;
Sing out thy notes on high
To sunbeam straying by
Or passing cloud;
    Heedless if thou art heard
Sing thy full song aloud.

Oh that it were with me
    As with the flower;
Blooming on its own tree
For butterfly and bee

Its summer morns:
        That I might bloom mine hour
A rose in spite of thorns.

Oh that my work were done
        As birds' that soar
Rejoicing in the sun:
That when my time is run
And daylight too,
        I so might rest once more
Cool with refreshing dew.

An Apple Gathering

I plucked pink blossoms from mine apple-tree
    And wore them all that evening in my hair:
Then in due season when I went to see
        I found no apples there.

With dangling basket all along the grass
    As I had come I went the selfsame track:
My neighbours mocked me while they saw me pass
        So empty-handed back.

Lilian and Lilias smiled in trudging by,
    Their heaped-up basket teased me like a jeer;
Sweet-voiced they sang beneath the sunset sky,
        Their mother's home was near.

Plump Gertrude passed me with her basket full,
    A stronger hand than hers helped it along;
A voice talked with her through the shadows cool
        More sweet to me than song.

Ah, Willie, Willie, was my love less worth
    Than apples with their green leaves piled above?
I counted rosiest apples on the earth
        Of far less worth than love.

So once it was with me you stooped to talk
    Laughing and listening in this very lane:

To think that by this way we used to walk
    We shall not walk again!

I let my neighbours pass me, ones and twos
    And groups; the latest said the night grew chill,
And hastened: but I loitered, while the dews
    Fell fast I loitered still.

Song

Two doves upon the selfsame branch,
    Two lilies on a single stem,
Two butterflies upon one flower:—
    Oh happy they who look on them.

Who look upon them hand in hand
    Flushed in the rosy summer light;
Who look upon them hand in hand
    And never give a thought to night.

Maude Clare

Out of the church she followed them
    With a lofty step and mien:
His bride was like a village maid,
    Maude Clare was like a queen.

"Son Thomas," his lady mother said,
    With smiles, almost with tears:
"May Nell and you but live as true
    As we have done for years;

"Your father thirty years ago
    Had just your tale to tell;
But he was not so pale as you,
    Nor I so pale as Nell."

My lord was pale with inward strife,
    And Nell was pale with pride;
My lord gazed long on pale Maude Clare
    Or ever he kissed the bride.

"Lo, I have brought my gift, my lord,
   Have brought my gift," she said:
"To bless the hearth, to bless the board,
   To bless the marriage-bed.

"Here's my half of the golden chain
   You wore about your neck,
That day we waded ankle-deep
   For lilies in the beck:

"Here's my half of the faded leaves
   We plucked from budding bough,
With feet amongst the lily leaves, —
   The lilies are budding now."

He strove to match her scorn with scorn,
   He faltered in his place:
"Lady," he said, — "Maude Clare," he said, —
   "Maude Clare": — and hid his face.

She turn'd to Nell: "My Lady Nell,
   I have a gift for you;
Though, were it fruit, the bloom were gone,
   Or, were it flowers, the dew.

"Take my share of a fickle heart,
   Mine of a paltry love:
Take it or leave it as you will,
   I wash my hands thereof."

"And what you leave," said Nell, "I'll take,
   And what you spurn, I'll wear;
For he's my lord for better and worse,
   And him I love, Maude Clare.

"Yea, though you're taller by the head,
   More wise and much more fair;
I'll love him till he loves me best,
   Me best of all, Maude Clare."

Echo

Come to me in the silence of the night;
   Come in the speaking silence of a dream:
Come with soft rounded cheeks and eyes as bright
   As sunlight on a stream;
     Come back in tears,
O memory, hope, love of finished years.

Oh dream how sweet, too sweet, too bitter sweet,
   Whose wakening should have been in Paradise,
Where souls brimfull of love abide and meet;
   Where thirsting longing eyes
     Watch the slow door
That opening, letting in, lets out no more.

Yet come to me in dreams, that I may live
   My very life again though cold in death:
Come back to me in dreams, that I may give
   Pulse for pulse, breath for breath:
     Speak low, lean low,
As long ago, my love, how long ago!

Winter: My Secret

I tell my secret? No indeed, not I:
Perhaps some day, who knows?
But not today; it froze, and blows, and snows,
And you're too curious: fie!
You want to hear it? well:
Only, my secret's mine, and I won't tell.

Or, after all, perhaps there's none:
Suppose there is no secret after all,
But only just my fun.
Today's a nipping day, a biting day;
In which one wants a shawl,
A veil, a cloak, and other wraps:
I cannot ope to every one who taps,
And let the draughts come whistling thro' my hall;
Come bounding and surrounding me,

Come buffeting, astounding me,
Nipping and clipping thro' my wraps and all.
I wear my mask for warmth: who ever shows
His nose to Russian snows
To be pecked at by every wind that blows?
You would not peck? I thank you for good will,
Believe, but leave that truth untested still.

Spring's an expansive time: yet I don't trust
March with its peck of dust,
Nor April with its rainbow-crowned brief showers,
Nor even May, whose flowers
One frost may wither thro' the sunless hours.

Perhaps some languid summer day,
When drowsy birds sing less and less,
And golden fruit is ripening to excess,
If there's not too much sun nor too much cloud,
And the warm wind is neither still nor loud,
Perhaps my secret I may say,
Or you may guess.

Another Spring

If I might see another Spring
    I'd not plant summer flowers and wait:
I'd have my crocuses at once,
My leafless pink mezereons,
    My chill-veined snowdrops, choicer yet
    My white or azure violet,
Leaf-nested primrose; anything
    To blow at once not late.

If I might see another Spring
    I'd listen to the daylight birds
That build their nests and pair and sing,
Nor wait for mateless nightingale;
    I'd listen to the lusty herds,
    The ewes with lambs as white as snow,
I'd find out music in the hail
    And all the winds that blow.

If I might see another Spring—
    Oh stinging comment on my past
That all my past results in "if"—
    If I might see another Spring
I'd laugh to-day, to-day is brief;
I would not wait for anything:
    I'd use to-day that cannot last,
    Be glad to-day and sing.

"No, Thank You, John"

I never said I loved you, John:
    Why will you tease me day by day,
And wax a weariness to think upon
    With always "do" and "pray"?

You know I never loved you, John;
    No fault of mine made me your toast:
Why will you haunt me with a face as wan
    As shows an hour-old ghost?

I dare say Meg or Moll would take
    Pity upon you, if you'd ask:
And pray don't remain single for my sake
    Who can't perform that task.

I have no heart?—Perhaps I have not;
    But then you're mad to take offence
That I don't give you what I have not got:
    Use your own common sense.

Let bygones be bygones:
    Don't call me false, who owed not to be true:
I'd rather answer "No" to fifty Johns
    Than answer "Yes" to you.

Let's mar our pleasant days no more,
    Song-birds of passage, days of youth:
Catch at today, forget the days before:
    I'll wink at your untruth.

Let us strike hands as hearty friends;
    No more, no less; and friendship's good:
Only don't keep in view ulterior ends,
        And points not understood

In open treaty. Rise above
    Quibbles and shuffling off and on:
Here's friendship for you if you like; but love,—
        No, thank you, John.

May

I cannot tell you how it was;
But this I know: it came to pass
Upon a bright and breezy day
When May was young; ah, pleasant May!
As yet the poppies were not born
Between the blades of tender corn;
The last eggs had not hatched as yet,
Nor any bird forgone its mate.

I cannot tell you what it was;
But this I know: it did but pass.
It passed away with sunny May,
With all sweet things it passed away,
And left me old, and cold, and grey.

A Pause of Thought

I looked for that which is not, nor can be,
    And hope deferred made my heart sick in truth:
    But years must pass before a hope of youth
        Is resigned utterly.

I watched and waited with a steadfast will:
    And though the object seemed to flee away
    That I so longed for, ever day by day
        I watched and waited still.

Sometimes I said: This thing shall be no more;
   My expectation wearies and shall cease;
   I will resign it now and be at peace:
      Yet never gave it o'er.

Sometimes I said: It is an empty name
   I long for; to a name why should I give
   The peace of all the days I have to live?—
      Yet gave it all the same.

Alas, thou foolish one! alike unfit
   For healthy joy and salutary pain:
   Thou knowest the chase useless, and again
      Turnest to follow it.

Song

When I am dead, my dearest,
   Sing no sad songs for me;
Plant thou no roses at my head,
   Nor shady cypress tree:
Be the green grass above me
   With showers and dewdrops wet;
And if thou wilt, remember,
   And if thou wilt, forget.

I shall not see the shadows,
   I shall not feel the rain;
I shall not hear the nightingale
   Sing on, as if in pain:
And dreaming through the twilight
   That doth not rise nor set,
Haply I may remember,
   And haply may forget.

Sister Maude

Who told my mother of my shame,
   Who told my father of my dear?
Oh who but Maude, my sister Maude,
   Who lurked to spy and peer.

Cold he lies, as cold as stone,
    With his clotted curls about his face:
The comeliest corpse in all the world
    And worthy of a queen's embrace.

You might have spared his soul, sister,
    Have spared my soul, your own soul too:
Though I had not been born at all,
    He'd never have looked at you.

My father may sleep in Paradise,
    My mother at Heaven-gate:
But sister Maude shall get no sleep
    Either early or late.

My father may wear a golden gown,
    My mother a crown may win;
If my dear and I knocked at Heaven-gate
    Perhaps they'd let us in:
But sister Maude, oh sister Maude,
    Bide *you* with death and sin.

The First Spring Day

I wonder if the sap is stirring yet,
If wintry birds are dreaming of a mate,
If frozen snowdrops feel as yet the sun
And crocus fires are kindling one by one:
        Sing, robin, sing;
I still am sore in doubt concerning Spring.

I wonder if the springtide of this year
Will bring another Spring both lost and dear;
If heart and spirit will find out their Spring,
Or if the world alone will bud and sing:
        Sing, hope, to me;
Sweet notes, my hope, soft notes for memory.

The sap will surely quicken soon or late,
The tardiest bird will twitter to a mate;
So Spring must dawn again with warmth and bloom,

Or in this world, or in the world to come:
    Sing, voice of Spring,
Till I too blossom and rejoice and sing.

The Convent Threshold

There's blood between us, love, my love,
There's father's blood, there's brother's blood;
And blood's a bar I cannot pass:
I choose the stairs that mount above,
Stair after golden skyward stair,
To city and to sea of glass.
My lily feet are soiled with mud,
With scarlet mud which tells a tale
Of hope that was, of guilt that was,
Of love that shall not yet avail;
Alas, my heart, if I could bare
My heart, this selfsame stain is there:
I seek the sea of glass and fire
To wash the spot, to burn the snare;
Lo, stairs are meant to lift us higher:
Mount with me, mount the kindled stair.

Your eyes look earthward, mine look up.
I see the far-off city grand,
Beyond the hills a watered land,
Beyond the gulf a gleaming strand
Of mansions where the righteous sup;
Who sleep at ease among their trees,
Or wake to sing a cadenced hymn
With Cherubim and Seraphim;
They bore the Cross, they drained the cup,
Racked, roasted, crushed, wrenched limb from limb,
They the offscouring of the world:
The heaven of starry heavens unfurled,
The sun before their face is dim.

You looking earthward what see you?
Milk-white wine-flushed among the vines,
Up and down leaping, to and fro,
Most glad, most full, made strong with wines,
Blooming as peaches pearled with dew,
Their golden windy hair afloat,

Love-music warbling in their throat,
Young men and women come and go.

You linger, yet the time is short:
Flee for your life, gird up your strength
To flee; the shadows stretched at length
Show that day wanes, that night draws nigh;
Flee to the mountain, tarry not.
Is this a time for smile and sigh,
For songs among the secret trees
Where sudden blue birds nest and sport?
The time is short and yet you stay:
To-day while it is called to-day
Kneel, wrestle, knock, do violence, pray;
To-day is short, to-morrow nigh:
Why will you die? why will you die?

You sinned with me a pleasant sin:
Repent with me, for I repent.
Woe's me the lore I must unlearn!
Woe's me that easy way we went,
So rugged when I would return!
How long until my sleep begin,
How long shall stretch these nights and days?
Surely, clean Angels cry, she prays;
She laves her soul with tedious tears:
How long must stretch these years and years?
I turn from you my cheeks and eyes,
My hair which you shall see no more—
Alas for joy that went before,
For joy that dies, for love that dies.
Only my lips still turn to you,
My livid lips that cry, Repent.
Oh weary life, oh weary Lent,
Oh weary time whose stars are few.

How should I rest in Paradise,
Or sit on steps of heaven alone?
If Saints and Angels spoke of love
Should I not answer from my throne:
Have pity upon me, ye my friends,
For I have heard the sound thereof:
Should I not turn with yearning eyes,
Turn earthwards with a pitiful pang?

Oh save me from a pang in heaven.
By all the gifts we took and gave,
Repent, repent, and be forgiven:
This life is long, but yet it ends;
Repent and purge your soul and save:
No gladder song the morning stars
Upon their birthday morning sang
Than Angels sing when one repents.

I tell you what I dreamed last night:
A spirit with transfigured face
Fire-footed clomb an infinite space.
I heard his hundred pinions clang,
Heaven-bells rejoicing rang and rang,
Heaven-air was thrilled with subtle scents
Worlds spun upon their rushing cars:
He mounted shrieking: "Give me light."
Still light was poured on him, more light;
Angels, Archangels he outstripped
Exultant in exceeding might,
And trod the skirts of Cherubim.
Still "Give me light," he shrieked; and dipped
His thirsty face, and drank a sea,
Athirst with thirst it could not slake.
I saw him, drunk with knowledge, take
From aching brows the aureole crown—
His locks writhed like a cloven snake—
He left his throne to grovel down
And lick the dust of Seraph's feet:
For what is knowledge duly weighed?
Knowledge is strong but love is sweet;
Yea all the progress ye had made
Was but to learn that all is small
Save love, for love is all in all.

I tell you what I dreamed last night:
It was not dark, it was not light,
Cold dews had drenched my plenteous hair
Through clay; you came to seek me there.
And "Do you dream of me?" you said.
My heart was dust that used to leap
To you; I answered half asleep:
"My pillow is damp, my sheets are red,

There's a leaden tester to my bed:
Find you a warmer playfellow,
A warmer pillow for your head,
A kinder love to love than mine."
You wrung your hands; while I like lead
Crushed downwards through the sodden earth:
You smote your hands but not in mirth,
And reeled but were not drunk with wine.

For all night long I dreamed of you:
I woke and prayed against my will,
Then slept to dream of you again.
At length I rose and knelt and prayed:
I cannot write the words I said,
My words were slow, my tears were few;
But through the dark my silence spoke
Like thunder. When this morning broke,
My face was pinched, my hair was grey,
And frozen blood was on the sill
Where stifling in my struggle I lay.

If now you saw me you would say:
Where is the face I used to love?
And I would answer: Gone before;
It tarries veiled in paradise.
When once the morning star shall rise,
When earth with shadow flees away
And we stand safe within the door,
Then you shall lift the veil thereof.
Look up, rise up: for far above
Our palms are grown, our place is set;
There we shall meet as once we met
And love with old familiar love.

Up-Hill

Does the road wind up-hill all the way?
    Yes, to the very end.
Will the day's journey take the whole long day?
    From morn to night, my friend.

But is there for the night a resting-place?
    A roof for when the slow dark hours begin.
May not the darkness hide it from my face?
    You cannot miss that inn.

Shall I meet other wayfarers at night?
    Those who have gone before.
Then must I knock, or call when just in sight?
    They will not keep you standing at that door.

Shall I find comfort, travel-sore and weak?
    Of labour you shall find the sum.
Will there be beds for me and all who seek?
    Yea, beds for all who come.

"A Bruised Reed Shall He Not Break"

I will accept thy will to do and be,
    Thy hatred and intolerance of sin,
    Thy will at least to love, that burns within
        And thirsteth after Me:
So will I render fruitful, blessing still,
    The germs and small beginnings in thy heart,
    Because thy will cleaves to the better part.—
        Alas, I cannot will.

Dost not thou will, poor soul? Yet I receive
    The inner unseen longings of the soul,
    I guide them turning towards Me; I control
        And charm hearts till they grieve:
If thou desire, it yet shall come to pass,
    Though thou but wish indeed to choose My love;
    For I have power in earth and heaven above.—
        I cannot wish, alas!

What, neither choose nor wish to choose? and yet
    I still must strive to win thee and constrain:
    For thee I hung upon the cross in pain,
        How then can I forget?
If thou as yet dost neither love, nor hate,

Nor choose, nor wish,—resign thyself, be still
Till I infuse love, hatred, longing, will.—
    I do not deprecate.

A Better Resurrection

I have no wit, no words, no tears;
    My heart within me like a stone
Is numbed too much for hopes or fears;
    Look right, look left, I dwell alone;
I lift mine eyes, but dimmed with grief
    No everlasting hills I see;
My life is in the falling leaf:
        O Jesus, quicken me.

My life is like a faded leaf,
    My harvest dwindled to a husk;
Truly my life is void and brief
    And tedious in the barren dusk;
    My life is like a frozen thing;
        No bud nor greenness can I see:
    Yet rise it shall—the sap of Spring;
        O Jesus, rise in me.

My life is like a broken bowl,
    A broken bowl that cannot hold
One drop of water for my soul
    Or cordial in the searching cold;
Cast in the fire the perished thing,
    Melt and remould it, till it be
A royal cup for Him my King:
        O Jesus, drink of me.

The Three Enemies

THE FLESH
"Sweet, thou art pale."
                        "More pale to see,
    Christ hung upon the cruel tree
    And bore His Father's wrath for me."

"Sweet, thou art sad."
                    "Beneath a rod
More heavy, Christ for my sake trod
The winepress of the wrath of God."

"Sweet, thou art weary."
                    "Not so Christ:
Whose mighty love of me sufficed
For Strength, Salvation, Eucharist."

"Sweet, thou art footsore."
                    "If I bleed,
His feet have bled: yea, in my need
His Heart once bled for mine indeed."

THE WORLD
"Sweet, thou art young."
                    "So He was young
Who for my sake in silence hung
Upon the Cross with Passion wrung."

"Look, thou art fair."
                    "He was more fair
Than men, Who deigned for me to wear
A visage marred beyond compare."

"And thou hast riches."
                    "Daily bread:
All else is His; Who living, dead,
For me lacked where to lay His Head."

"And life is sweet."
                    "It was not so
To Him, Whose cup did overflow
With mine unutterable woe."

THE DEVIL
"Thou drinkest deep."
                    "When Christ would sup
He drained the dregs from out my cup:
So how should I be lifted up?"

"Thou shalt win Glory."
                         "In the skies,
Lord Jesus, cover up mine eyes
Lest they should look on vanities."

"Thou shalt have Knowledge."
                              "Helpless dust!
In Thee, O Lord, I put my trust:
Answer Thou for me, Wise and Just."

"And Might." —
                    "Get thee behind me. Lord,
Who hast redeemed and not abhorred
My soul, oh keep it by Thy Word."

The One Certainty

SONNET

Vanity of vanities, the Preacher saith,
  All things are vanity. The eye and ear
  Cannot be filled with what they see and hear.
Like early dew, or like the sudden breath
Of wind, or like the grass that withereth,
  Is man, tossed to and fro by hope and fear:
  So little joy hath he, so little cheer,
Till all things end in the long dust of death.
To-day is still the same as yesterday,
  To-morrow also even as one of them;
And there is nothing new under the sun:
Until the ancient race of Time be run,
  The old thorns shall grow out of the old stem,
And morning shall be cold and twilight grey.

Sweet Death

The sweetest blossoms die.
  And so it was that, going day by day
  Unto the Church to praise and pray,
And crossing the green churchyard thoughtfully,
  I saw how on the graves the flowers

Shed their fresh leaves in showers,
And how their perfume rose up to the sky
    Before it passed away.

The youngest blossoms die.
    They die and fall and nourish the rich earth
    From which they lately had their birth;
Sweet life, but sweeter death that passeth by
    And is as though it had not been:—
    All colours turn to green;
The bright hues vanish and the odours fly,
    The grass hath lasting worth.

And youth and beauty die.
    So be it, O my God, Thou God of truth:
    Better than beauty and than youth
Are Saints and Angels, a glad company;
    And Thou, O Lord, our Rest and Ease,
    Art better far than these.
Why should we shrink from our full harvest? why
    Prefer to glean with Ruth?

The World

SONNET

By day she woos me, soft, exceeding fair:
    But all night as the moon so changeth she;
    Loathsome and foul with hideous leprosy
And subtle serpents gliding in her hair.
By day she woos me to the outer air,
    Ripe fruit, sweet flowers, and full satiety:
    But through the night, a beast she grins at me,
A very monster void of love and prayer.
By day she stands a lie: by night she stands
    In all the naked horror of the truth
With pushing horns and clawed and clutching hands.
Is this a friend indeed; that I should sell
    My soul to her, give her my life and youth,
Till my feet, cloven too, take hold on hell?

Spring Quiet

Gone were but the Winter,
    Come were but the Spring,
I would go to a covert
    Where the birds sing;

Where in the whitethorn
    Singeth a thrush,
And a robin sings
    In the holly-bush.

Full of fresh scents
    Are the budding boughs
Arching high over
    A cool green house:

Full of sweet scents,
    And whispering air
Which sayeth softly:
    "We spread no snare;

"Here dwell in safety,
    Here dwell alone,
With a clear stream
    And a mossy stone.

"Here the sun shineth
    Most shadily;
Here is heard an echo
    Of the far sea,
        Though far off it be."

A Portrait

I
She gave up beauty in her tender youth,
    Gave up all hope and joy and pleasant ways;
    She covered up her eyes lest they should gaze
On vanity, and chose the bitter truth.
Harsh towards herself, towards others full of ruth,
    Servants of servants, little known to praise,
    Long prayers and fasts trenched on her nights and days:

She schooled herself to sights and sounds uncouth
That with the poor and stricken she might make
   A home, until the least of all sufficed
Her wants; her own self learned she to forsake,
Counting all earthly gain but hurt and loss.
So with calm will she chose and bore the cross
   And hated all for love of Jesus Christ.

II
They knelt in silent anguish by her bed,
   And could not weep; but calmly there she lay.
   All pain had left her; and the sun's last ray
Shone through upon her, warming into red
The shady curtains. In her heart she said:
   "Heaven opens; I leave these and go away;
   The Bridegroom calls,—shall the Bride seek to stay?"
Then low upon her breast she bowed her head.
O lily flower, O gem of priceless worth,
   O dove with patient voice and patient eyes,
O fruitful vine amid a land of dearth,
   O maid replete with loving purities,
Thou bowedst down thy head with friends on earth
   To raise it with the saints in Paradise.

Dream-Love

Young Love lies sleeping
   In May-time of the year,
Among the lilies,
   Lapped in the tender light:
White lambs come grazing,
   White doves come building there;
And round about him
   The May-bushes are white.

Soft moss the pillow
   For oh, a softer cheek;
Broad leaves cast shadow
   Upon the heavy eyes:
There winds and waters
   Grow lulled and scarcely speak;

There twilight lingers
   The longest in the skies.

Young Love lies dreaming;
   But who shall tell the dream?
A perfect sunlight
   On rustling forest tips;
Or perfect moonlight
   Upon a rippling stream;
Or perfect silence,
   Or song of cherished lips.

Burn odours round him
   To fill the drowsy air;
Weave silent dances
   Around him to and fro;
For oh, in waking
   The sights are not so fair,
And song and silence
   Are not like these below.

Young Love lies dreaming
   Till summer days are gone,—
Dreaming and drowsing
   Away to perfect sleep:
He sees the beauty
   Sun hath not looked upon,
And tastes the fountain
   Unutterably deep.

Him perfect music
   Doth hush unto his rest,
And through the pauses
   The perfect silence calms:
Oh, poor the voices
   Of earth from east to west,
And poor earth's stillness
   Between her stately palms.

Young Love lies drowsing
   Away to poppied death;
Cool shadows deepen
   Across the sleeping face:

So fails the summer
    With warm, delicious breath;
And what hath autumn
    To give us in its place?

Draw close the curtains
    Of branched evergreen;
Change cannot touch them
    With fading fingers sere:
Here the first violets
    Perhaps will bud unseen,
And a dove, may be,
    Return to nestle here.

Twice

I took my heart in my hand
    (O my love, O my love),
I said: Let me fall or stand,
    Let me live or die,
But this once hear me speak—
    (O my love, O my love)—
Yet a woman's words are weak;
    You should speak, not I.

You took my heart in your hand
    With a friendly smile,
With a critical eye you scanned,
    Then set it down,
And said: It is still unripe,
    Better wait awhile;
Wait while the skylarks pipe,
    Till the corn grows brown.

As you set it down it broke—
    Broke, but I did not wince;
I smiled at the speech you spoke,
    At your judgment that I heard:
But I have not often smiled
    Since then, nor questioned since,
Nor cared for corn-flowers wild,
    Nor sung with the singing bird.

I take my heart in my hand,
    O my God, O my God,
My broken heart in my hand:
    Thou hast seen, judge Thou.
My hope was written on sand,
    O my God, O my God:
Now let Thy judgment stand—
    Yea, judge me now.

This contemned of a man,
    This marred one heedless day,
This heart take Thou to scan
    Both within and without:
Refine with fire its gold,
    Purge Thou its dross away—
Yea, hold it in Thy hold,
    Whence none can pluck it out.

I take my heart in my hand—
    I shall not die, but live—
Before Thy face I stand;
    I, for Thou callest such:
All that I have I bring,
    All that I am I give,
Smile Thou and I shall sing,
    But shall not question much.

One Day

I will tell you when they met:
In the limpid days of Spring;
Elder boughs were budding yet,
Oaken boughs looked wintry still,
But primrose and veined violet
In the mossful turf were set,
While meeting birds made haste to sing
And build with right good will.

I will tell you when they parted:
When plenteous Autumn sheaves were brown,
Then they parted heavy-hearted;
The full rejoicing sun looked down
As grand as in the days before;

Only they had lost a crown;
Only to them those days of yore
Could come back nevermore.

When shall they meet? I cannot tell,
Indeed, when they shall meet again,
Except some day in Paradise:
For this they wait, one waits in pain.
Beyond the sea of death love lies
For ever, yesterday, to-day;
Angels shall ask them, "Is it well?"
And they shall answer, "Yea."

A Dream

SONNET

Once in a dream (for once I dreamed of you)
  We stood together in an open field;
  Above our heads two swift-winged pigeons wheeled,
Sporting at ease and courting full in view.
When loftier still a broadening darkness flew,
  Down-swooping, and a ravenous hawk revealed;
  Too weak to fight, too fond to fly, they yield;
So farewell life and love and pleasures new.
Then as their plumes fell fluttering to the ground,
    Their snow-white plumage flecked with crimson drops,
      I wept, and thought I turned towards you to weep:
    But you were gone; while rustling hedgerow tops
Bent in a wind which bore to me a sound
    Of far-off piteous bleat of lambs and sheep.

Beauty Is Vain

While roses are so red,
  While lilies are so white,
Shall a woman exalt her face
  Because it gives delight?
She's not so sweet as a rose,

A lily's straighter than she,
And if she were as red or white
    She'd be but one of three.

Whether she flush in love's summer
    Or in its winter grow pale,
Whether she flaunt her beauty
    Or hide it away in a veil,
Be she red or white,
    And stand she erect or bowed,
Time will win the race he runs with her
    And hide her away in a shroud.

What Would I Give?

What would I give for a heart of flesh to warm me through,
Instead of this heart of stone ice-cold whatever I do;
Hard and cold and small, of all hearts the worst of all.

What would I give for words, if only words would come;
But now in its misery my spirit has fallen dumb:
Oh, merry friends, go your way, I have never a word to say.

What would I give for tears, not smiles but scalding tears,
To wash the black mark clean, and to thaw the frost of years,
To wash the stain ingrain and to make me clean again.

The Bourne

Underneath the growing grass,
    Underneath the living flowers,
    Deeper than the sound of showers:
    There we shall not count the hours
By the shadows as they pass.

Youth and health will be but vain,
    Beauty reckoned of no worth:
    There a very little girth
    Can hold round what once the earth
Seemed too narrow to contain.

Memory

I

I nursed it in my bosom while it lived,
   I hid it in my heart when it was dead;
In joy I sat alone, even so I grieved
    Alone and nothing said.

I shut the door to face the naked truth,
   I stood alone—I faced the truth alone,
Stripped bare of self-regard or forms or ruth
    Till first and last were shown.

I took the perfect balances and weighed;
   No shaking of my hand disturbed the poise;
Weighed, found it wanting: not a word I said,
    But silent made my choice.

None know the choice I made; I make it still.
   None know the choice I made and broke my heart,
Breaking mine idol: I have braced my will
    Once, chosen for once my part.

I broke it at a blow, I laid it cold,
   Crushed in my deep heart where it used to live.
My heart dies inch by inch; the time grows old,
    Grows old in which I grieve.

II

I have a room whereinto no one enters
   Save I myself alone:
   There sits a blessed memory on a throne,
There my life centres.

While winter comes and goes—oh tedious comer!—
   And while its nip-wind blows;
   While bloom the bloodless lily and warm rose
Of lavish summer.

If any should force entrance he might see there
   One buried yet not dead,
   Before whose face I no more bow my head
Or bend my knee there;

But often in my worn life's autumn weather
   I watch there with clear eyes,
   And think how it will be in Paradise
When we're together.

Shall I Forget?

Shall I forget on this side of the grave?
I promise nothing: you must wait and see
   Patient and brave.
 (O my soul, watch with him and he with me.)

Shall I forget in peace of Paradise?
I promise nothing: follow, friend, and see
   Faithful and wise.
 (O my soul, lead the way he walks with me.)

Vanity of Vanities

SONNET

Ah, woe is me for pleasure that is vain,
   Ah, woe is me for glory that is past:
   Pleasure that bringeth sorrow at the last,
Glory that at the last bringeth no gain!
So saith the sinking heart; and so again
   It shall say till the mighty angel-blast
   Is blown, making the sun and moon aghast
And showering down the stars like sudden rain.
And evermore men shall go fearfully
   Bending beneath their weight of heaviness;
And ancient men shall lie down wearily,
   And strong men shall rise up in weariness;
Yea, even the young shall answer sighingly
   Saying one to another: How vain it is!

L.E.L.

"Whose heart was breaking for a little love."

Downstairs I laugh, I sport and jest with all:
    But in my solitary room above
I turn my face in silence to the wall;
    My heart is breaking for a little love.
        Though winter frosts are done,
        And birds pair every one,
And leaves peep out, for springtide is begun.

I feel no spring, while spring is wellnigh blown,
    I find no nest, while nests are in the grove:
Woe's me for mine own heart that dwells alone,
    My heart that breaketh for a little love.
        While golden in the sun
        Rivulets rise and run,
While lilies bud, for springtide is begun.

All love, are loved, save only I; their hearts
    Beat warm with love and joy, beat full thereof;
They cannot guess, who play the pleasant parts,
    My heart is breaking for a little love.
        While beehives wake and whirr,
        And rabbit thins his fur,
In living spring that sets the world astir.

I deck myself with silks and jewelry,
    I plume myself like any mated dove:
They praise my rustling show, and never see
    My heart is breaking for a little love.
        While sprouts green lavender
        With rosemary and myrrh,
For in quick spring the sap is all astir.

Perhaps some saints in glory guess the truth,
    Perhaps some angels read it as they move,
And cry one to another full of ruth,
    "Her heart is breaking for a little love."
        Though other things have birth,
        And leap and sing for mirth,
When springtime wakes and clothes and feeds the earth.

Yet saith a saint: "Take patience for thy scathe";
   Yet saith an angel: "Wait, for thou shalt prove
True best is last, true life is born of death,
   O thou, heart-broken for a little love.
     Then love shall fill thy girth,
     And love make fat thy dearth,
When new spring builds new heaven and clean new earth."

Life and Death

Life is not sweet. One day it will be sweet
   To shut our eyes and die:
Nor feel the wild flowers blow, nor birds dart by
   With flitting butterfly,
Nor grass grow long above our heads and feet,
Nor hear the happy lark that soars sky high,
   Nor sigh that spring is fleet and summer fleet,
   Nor mark the waxing wheat,
Nor know who sits in our accustomed seat.

Life is not good. One day it will be good
   To die, then live again;
To sleep meanwhile: so not to feel the wane
Of shrunk leaves dropping in the wood,
Nor hear the foamy lashing of the main,
Nor mark the blackened bean-fields, nor where stood
   Rich ranks of golden grain
Only dead refuse stubble clothe the plain:
Asleep from risk, asleep from pain.

Grown and Flown

I loved my love from green of Spring
   Until sere Autumn's fall;
But now that leaves are withering
   How should one love at all?
   One heart's too small
For hunger, cold, love, everything.

I loved my love on sunny days
   Until late Summer's wane;
But now that frost begins to glaze

How should one love again?
　　Nay, love and pain
Walk wide apart in diverse ways.

I loved my love—alas to see
　　That this should be, alas!
I thought that this could scarcely be,
　　Yet has it come to pass:
　　Sweet sweet love was,
Now bitter bitter grown to me.

Despised and Rejected

My sun has set, I dwell
In darkness as a dead man out of sight;
And none remains, not one, that I should tell
To him mine evil plight
This bitter night.
I will make fast my door
That hollow friends may trouble me no more.

"Friend, open to Me."—Who is this that calls?
Nay, I am deaf as are my walls:
Cease crying, for I will not hear
Thy cry of hope or fear.
Others were dear,
Others forsook me: what art thou indeed
That I should heed
Thy lamentable need?
Hungry should feed,
Or stranger lodge thee here?

"Friend, My Feet bleed.
Open thy door to Me and comfort Me."
I will not open, trouble me no more.
Go on thy way footsore,
I will not rise and open unto thee.
"Then is it nothing to thee? Open, see
Who stands to plead with thee.
Open, lest I should pass thee by, and thou
One day entreat My Face

And howl for grace,
And I be deaf as thou art now.
Open to Me."

Then I cried out upon him: Cease,
Leave me in peace:
Fear not that I should crave
Aught thou mayst have.
Leave me in peace, yea trouble me no more,
Lest I arise and chase thee from my door.
What, shall I not be let
Alone, that thou dost vex me yet?

But all night long that voice spake urgently:
"Open to Me."
Still harping in mine ears:
"Rise, let Me in."
Pleading with tears:
"Open to Me that I may come to thee."
While the dew dropped, while the dark hours were cold:
"My Feet bleed, see My Face,
See My Hands bleed that bring thee grace,
My Heart doth bleed for thee,
Open to Me."

So till the break of day:
Then died away
That voice, in silence as of sorrow;
Then footsteps echoing like a sigh
Passed me by,
Lingering footsteps slow to pass.
On the morrow
I saw upon the grass
Each footprint marked in blood, and on my door
The mark of blood for evermore.

The Lowest Place

Give me the lowest place: not that I dare
    Ask for that lowest place, but Thou hast died
That I might live and share
    Thy glory by Thy side.

Give me the lowest place: or if for me
   That lowest place too high, make one more low
Where I may sit and see
   My God and love Thee so.

Consider

     Consider
The lilies of the field whose bloom is brief:—
     We are as they;
     Like them we fade away,
As doth a leaf.

     Consider
The sparrows of the air of small account:
     Our God doth view
Whether they fall or mount,—
     He guards us too.

     Consider
The lilies that do neither spin nor toil,
     Yet are most fair:—
     What profits all this care
And all this coil?

     Consider
The birds that have no barn nor harvest-weeks;
     God gives them food:—
Much more our Father seeks
     To do us good.

A Smile and a Sigh

A smile because the nights are short!
   And every morning brings such pleasure
Of sweet love-making, harmless sport:
   Love, that makes and finds its treasure;
   Love, treasure without measure.

A sigh because the days are long!
   Long long these days that pass in sighing,
A burden saddens every song:
   While time lags who should be flying,
   We live who would be dying.

Paradise: In a Dream

Once in a dream I saw the flowers
   That bud and bloom in Paradise;
   More fair they are than waking eyes
Have seen in all this world of ours.
And faint the perfume-bearing rose,
   And faint the lily on its stem,
And faint the perfect violet
      Compared with them.

I heard the songs of Paradise:
   Each bird sat singing in his place;
   A tender song so full of grace
It soared like incense to the skies.
Each bird sat singing to his mate
   Soft cooing notes among the trees:
The nightingale herself were cold
      To such as these.

I saw the fourfold River flow,
   And deep it was, with golden sand;
   It flowed between a mossy land
With murmured music grave and low.
It hath refreshment for all thirst,
   For fainting spirits strength and rest;
Earth holds not such a draught as this
      From east to west.

The Tree of Life stood budding there,
   Abundant with its twelvefold fruits;
   Eternal sap sustains its roots,
Its shadowing branches fill the air.

Its leaves are healing for the world,
    Its fruit the hungry world can feed,
Sweeter than honey to the taste
        And balm indeed.

I saw the gate called Beautiful;
    And looked, but scarce could look within;
    I saw the golden streets begin,
And outskirts of the glassy pool.
Oh harps, oh crowns of plenteous stars,
    Oh green palm branches many-leaved—
Eye hath not seen, nor ear hath heard,
        Nor heart conceived.

I hope to see these things again,
    But not as once in dreams by night;
    To see them with my very sight,
And touch and handle and attain:
To have all Heaven beneath my feet
    For narrow way that once they trod;
To have my part with all the saints,
        And with my God.

Sleeping at Last

Sleeping at last, the trouble and tumult over,
    Sleeping at last, the struggle and horror past,
Cold and white, out of sight of friend and of lover,
        Sleeping at last.

No more a tired heart downcast or overcast,
No more pangs that wring or shifting fears that hover,
    Sleeping at last in a dreamless sleep locked fast.

Fast asleep. Singing birds in their leafy cover
    Cannot wake her, nor shake her the gusty blast.
Under the purple thyme and the purple clover
        Sleeping at last.

ALGERNON CHARLES SWINBURNE
(1837–1909)

Often remembered for the dissipation and vices that nearly destroyed him, Swinburne was nevertheless one of the major nineteenth-century English poets, a master of poetic meter and an iconoclastic sensualist whose passionate verse shocked contemporary readers. He was "the poet of youth insurgent against all the restraints of conventionality and custom." In addition to the passion and fervor of his verse, Swinburne's technical innovations helped release English poetry from the constraints of formalism. Overall, his metrical ingenuity, devotion to poetry, and formidable artistic personality had a profound impact on the development of English lyric poetry.

The Garden of Proserpine

Here, where the world is quiet;
   Here, where all trouble seems
Dead winds' and spent waves' riot
   In doubtful dreams of dreams;
I watch the green field growing
For reaping folk and sowing,
For harvest-time and mowing,
   A sleepy world of streams.

I am tired of tears and laughter,
   And men that laugh and weep,
Of what may come hereafter
   For men that sow to reap;
I am weary of days and hours,

Blown buds of barren flowers,
. Desires and dreams and powers
　　And everything but sleep.

Here life has death for neighbor,
　　And far from eye or ear
Wan waves and wet winds labor,
　　Weak ships and spirits steer;
They drive adrift, and whither
They wot not who make thither;
But no such winds blow hither,
　　And no such things grow here.

No growth of moor or coppice,
　　No heather-flower or vine,
But bloomless buds of poppies,
　　Green grapes of Proserpine,
Pale beds of blowing rushes
Where no leaf blooms or blushes
Save this whereout she crushes
　　For dead men deadly wine.

Pale, without name or number,
　　In fruitless fields of corn,
They bow themselves and slumber
　　All night till light is born;
And like a soul belated,
In hell and heaven unmated,
By cloud and mist abated
　　Comes out of darkness morn.

Though one were strong as seven,
　　He too with death shall dwell,
Nor wake with wings in heaven,
　　Nor weep for pains in hell;
Though one were fair as roses,
His beauty clouds and closes;
And well though love reposes,
　　In the end it is not well.

Pale, beyond porch and portal,
　　Crowned with calm leaves, she stands
Who gathers all things mortal

With cold immortal hands;
Her languid lips are sweeter
Than love's who fears to greet her
To men that mix and meet her
    From many times and lands.

She waits for each and other,
    She waits for all men born;
Forgets the earth her mother,
    The life of fruits and corn;
And spring and seed and swallow
Take wing for her and follow
Where summer song rings hollow
    And flowers are put to scorn.

There go the loves that wither,
    The old loves with wearier wings;
And all dead years draw thither,
    And all disastrous things;
Dead dreams of days forsaken,
Blind buds that snows have shaken,
Wild leaves that winds have taken,
    Red strays of ruined springs.

We are not sure of sorrow,
    And joy was never sure;
Today will die tomorrow;
    Time stoops to no man's lure;
And love, grown faint and fretful,
With lips but half regretful
Sighs, and with eyes forgetful
    Weeps that no loves endure.

From too much love of living,
    From hope and fear set free,
We thank with brief thanksgiving
    Whatever gods may be
That no life lives forever;
That dead men rise up never;
That even the weariest river
    Winds somewhere safe to sea.

Then star nor sun shall waken,
   Nor any change of light;
Nor sound of waters shaken,
   Nor any sound or sight;
Nor wintry leaves nor vernal,
Not days nor things diurnal;
Only the sleep eternal
   In an eternal night.

Hymn to Proserpine

(AFTER THE PROCLAMATION IN ROME OF THE CHRISTIAN FAITH)

VICISTI, GALILAEE.

I have lived long enough, having seen one thing, that love hath an end;
Goddess and maiden and queen, be near me now and befriend.
Thou art more than the day or the morrow, the seasons that laugh or
   that weep;
For these give joy and sorrow; but thou, Proserpina, sleep.
Sweet is the treading of wine, and sweet the feet of the dove;
But a goodlier gift is thine than foam of the grapes or love.
Yea, is not even Apollo, with hair and harpstring of gold,
A bitter God to follow, a beautiful God to behold?
I am sick of singing: the bays burn deep and chafe: I am fain
To rest a little from praise and grievous pleasure and pain.
For the Gods we know not of, who give us our daily breath,
We know they are cruel as love or life, and lovely as death.
O Gods dethroned and deceased, cast forth, wiped out in a day!
From your wrath is the world released, redeem'd from your chains,
   men say.
New Gods are crown'd in the city; their flowers have broken your rods;
They are merciful, clothed with pity, the young compassionate Gods.
But for me their new device is barren, the days are bare;
Things long past over suffice, and men forgotten that were.
Time and the Gods are at strife; ye dwell in the midst thereof,
Draining a little life from the barren breasts of love.
I say to you, cease, take rest; yea, I say to you all, be at peace,
Till the bitter milk of her breast and the barren bosom shall cease.
Wilt thou yet take all, Galilean? but these thou shalt not take,
The laurel, the palms and the paean, the breasts of the nymphs in the
   brake;

Breasts more soft than a dove's, that tremble with tenderer breath;
And all the wings of the Loves, and all the joy before death;
All the feet of the hours that sound as a single lyre,
Dropp'd and deep in the flowers, with strings that flicker like fire.
More than these wilt thou give, things fairer than all these things?
Nay, for a little we live, and life hath mutable wings.
A little while and we die; shall life not thrive as it may?
For no man under the sky lives twice, outliving his day.
And grief is a grievous thing, and a man hath enough of his tears:
Why should he labour, and bring fresh grief to blacken his years?
Thou hast conquer'd, O pale Galilean; the world has grown grey from
    thy breath;
We have drunken of things Lethean, and fed on the fullness of death.
Laurel is green for a season, and love is sweet for a day;
But love grows bitter with treason, and laurel outlives not May.
Sleep, shall we sleep after all? for the world is not sweet in the end;
For the old faiths loosen and fall, the new years ruin and rend.
Fate is a sea without shore, and the soul is a rock that abides;
But her ears are vex'd with the roar and her face with the foam of the
    tides.
O lips that the live blood faints in, the leavings of racks and rods!
O ghastly glories of saints, dead limbs of gibbeted Gods!
Though all men abase them before you in spirit, and all knees bend,
I kneel not, neither adore you, but standing, look to the end.
All delicate days and pleasant, all spirits and sorrows are cast
Far out with the foam of the present that sweeps to the surf of the past:
Where beyond the extreme sea-wall, and between the remote sea-gates,
Waste water washes, and tall ships founder, and deep death waits:
Where, mighty with deepening sides, clad about with the seas as with
    wings,
And impell'd of invisible tides, and fulfill'd of unspeakable things,
White-eyed and poisonous-finn'd, shark-tooth'd and serpentine-curl'd,
Rolls, under the whitening wind of the future, the wave of the world.
The depths stand naked in sunder behind it, the storms flee away;
In the hollow before it the thunder is taken and snared as a prey;
In its sides is the north-wind bound; and its salt is of all men's tears;
With light of ruin, and sound of changes, and pulse of years:
With travail of day after day, and with trouble of hour upon hour;
And bitter as blood is the spray; and the crests are as fangs that devour:
And its vapour and storm of its steam as the sighing of spirits to be;
And its noise as the noise in a dream; and its depth as the roots of the
    sea:
And the height of its heads as the height of the utmost stars of the air:

And the ends of the earth at the might thereof tremble, and time is
  made bare.
Will ye bridle the deep sea with reins, will ye chasten the high sea with
  rods?
Will ye take her to chain her with chains, who is older than all ye
  Gods?
All ye as a wind shall go by, as a fire shall ye pass and be past;
Ye are Gods, and behold, ye shall die, and the waves be upon you at
  last.
In the darkness of time, in the deeps of the years, in the changes of
  things,
Ye shall sleep as a slain man sleeps, and the world shall forget you for
  kings.
Though the feet of thine high priests tread where thy lords and our
  forefathers trod,
Though these that were Gods are dead, and thou being dead art a God,
Though before thee the throned Cytherean be fallen, and hidden her
  head,
Yet thy kingdom shall pass, Galilean, thy dead shall go down to thee
  dead.
Of the maiden thy mother men sing as a goddess with grace clad
  around;
Thou art throned where another was king; where another was queen
  she is crown'd.
Yea, once we had sight of another: but now she is queen, say these.
Not as thine, not as thine was our mother, a blossom of flowering seas,
Clothed round with the world's desire as with raiment, and fair as the
  foam,
And fleeter than kindled fire, and a goddess, and mother of Rome.
For thine came pale and a maiden, and sister to sorrow; but ours,
Her deep hair heavily laden with odour and colour of flowers,
White rose of the rose-white water, a silver splendour, a flame,
Bent down unto us that besought her, and earth grew sweet with her
  name.
For thine came weeping, a slave among slaves, and rejected; but she
Came flush'd from the full-flush'd wave, and imperial her foot on the
  sea.
And the wonderful waters knew her, the winds and the viewless ways,
And the roses grew rosier, and bluer the sea-blue stream of the bays.
Ye are fallen, our lords, by what token? we wist that ye should not fall.
Ye were all so fair that are broken; and one more fair than ye all.
But I turn to her still, having seen she shall surely abide in the end;
Goddess and maiden and queen, be near me now and befriend.

O daughter of earth, of my mother, her crown and blossom of birth,
I am also, I also, thy brother; I go as I come unto earth.
In the night where thine eyes are as moons are in heaven, the night
where thou art,
Where the silence is more than all tunes, where sleep overflows from
the heart,
Where the poppies are sweet as the rose in our world, and the red rose
is white,
And the wind falls faint as it blows with the fume of the flowers of the
night,
And the murmur of spirits that sleep in the shadow of Gods from afar
Grows dim in thine ears and deep as the deep dim soul of a star,
In the sweet low light of thy face, under heavens untrod by the sun,
Let my soul with their souls find place, and forget what is done and
undone.
Thou art more than the Gods who number the days of our temporal
breath;
For these give labour and slumber; but thou, Proserpina, death.
Therefore now at thy feet I abide for a season in silence. I know
I shall die as my fathers died, and sleep as they sleep; even so.
For the glass of the years is brittle wherein we gaze for a span;
A little soul for a little bears up this corpse which is man.
So long I endure, no longer; and laugh not again, neither weep.
For there is no God found stronger than death; and death is a sleep.

Chorus from "Atalanta"

Before the beginning of years
    There came to the making of man
Time, with a gift of tears;
    Grief, with a glass that ran;
Pleasure, with pain for leaven;
    Summer, with flowers that fell;
Remembrance fallen from heaven,
    And madness risen from hell;
Strength without hands to smite;
    Love that endures for a breath;
Night, the shadow of light,
    And life, the shadow of death.

And the high gods took in hand
    Fire, and the falling of tears,

And a measure of sliding sand
   From under the feet of the years;
And froth and drift of the sea;
   And dust of the labouring earth;
And bodies of things to be
   In the houses of death and of birth;
And wrought with weeping and laughter,
   And fashion'd with loathing and love,
With life before and after
   And death beneath and above,
For a day and a night and a morrow,
   That his strength might endure for a span
With travail and heavy sorrow,
   The holy spirit of man.

From the winds of the north and the south
   They gather'd as unto strife;
They breathed upon his mouth,
   They fill'd his body with life;
Eyesight and speech they wrought
   For the veils of the soul therein,
A time for labour and thought,
   A time to serve and to sin;
They gave him light in his ways,
   And love, and a space for delight,
And beauty and length of days,
   And night, and sleep in the night.
His speech is a burning fire;
   With his lips he travaileth;
In his heart is a blind desire,
   In his eyes foreknowledge of death;

He weaves, and is clothed with derision;
   Sows, and he shall not reap;
His life is a watch or a vision
   Between a sleep and a sleep.

Super Flumina Babylonis

By the waters of Babylon we sat down and wept,
   Remembering thee,
That for ages of agony hast endured, and slept,
   And wouldst not see.

By the waters of Babylon we stood up and sang,
  Considering thee,
That a blast of deliverance in the darkness rang,
  To set thee free.

And with trumpets and thunderings and with morning song
  Came up the light;
And thy spirit uplifted thee to forget thy wrong
  As day doth night.

And thy sons were dejected not any more, as then
  When thou wast shamed;
When thy lovers went heavily without heart, as men
  Whose life was maim'd.

In the desolate distances, with a great desire,
  For thy love's sake,
With our hearts going back to thee, they were fill'd with fire,
  Were nigh to break.

It was said to us: "Verily ye are great of heart,
  But ye shall bend;
Ye are bondmen and bondwomen, to be scourged and smart,
  To toil and tend."

And with harrows men harrow'd us, and subdued with spears,
  And crush'd with shame;
And the summer and winter was, and the length of years,
  And no change came.

By the rivers of Italy, by the sacred streams,
  By town, by tower,
There was feasting with revelling, there was sleep with dreams,
  Until thine hour.

And they slept and they rioted on their rose-hung beds,
  With mouths on flame,
And with love-locks vine-chapleted, and with rose-crown'd heads
  And robes of shame.

And they knew not their forefathers, nor the hills and streams
  And words of power,

Nor the gods that were good to them, but with songs and dreams
    Fill'd up their hour.

By the rivers of Italy, by the dry streams' beds,
    When thy time came,
There was casting of crowns from them, from their young men's
  heads,
    The crowns of shame.

By the horn of Eridanus, by the Tiber mouth,
    As thy day rose,
They arose up and girded them to the north and south,
    By seas, by snows.

As a water in January the frost confines,
    Thy kings bound thee;
As a water in April is, in the new-blown vines,
    Thy sons made free.

And thy lovers that look'd for thee, and that morn'd from far,
    For thy sake dead,
We rejoiced in the light of thee, in the signal star
    Above thine head.

In thy grief had we follow'd thee, in thy passion loved,
    Loved in thy loss;
In thy shame we stood fast to thee, with thy pangs were moved,
    Clung to thy cross.

By the hillside of Calvary we beheld thy blood,
    Thy blood-red tears,
As a mother's in bitterness, and unebbing flood,
    Years upon years.

And the north was Gethsemane, without leaf or bloom,
    A garden seal'd;
And the south was Aceldama, for a sanguine fume
    Hid all the field.

By the stone of the sepulchre we return'd to weep,
    From far, from prison;
And the guards by it keeping it we beheld asleep,
    But thou wast risen.

And an angel's smilitude by the unseal'd grave,
    And by the stone:
And the voice was angelical, to whose words God gave
    Strength like his own.

"Lo, the graveclothes of Italy that are folded up
    In the grave's gloom!
And the guards as men wrought upon with a charmèd cup,
    By the open tomb.

"And her body most beautiful, and her shining head,
    These are not here;
For your mother, for Italy, is not surely dead:
    Have ye no fear.

"As of old time she spake to you, and you hardly heard,
    Hardly took heed,
So now also she saith to you, yet another word,
    Who is risen indeed.

"By my saying she saith to you, in your ears she saith,
    Who hear these things,
Put no trust in men's royalties, nor in great men's breath,
    Nor words of kings.

"For the life of them vanishes and is no more seen,
    Nor no more known;
Nor shall any remember him if a crown hath been,
    Or where a throne.

"Unto each man his handiwork, unto each his crown,
    The just Fate gives;
Whoso takes the world's life on him and his own lays down,
    He, dying so, lives.

"Whoso bears the whole heaviness of the wrong'd world's weight
    And puts it by,
It is well with him suffering, though he face man's fate;
    How should he die?

"Seeing death has no part in him any more, no power
    Upon his head;
He has brought his eternity with a little hour,
    And is not dead.

"For an hour if ye look for him, he is no more found,
    For one hour's space;
Then ye lift up your eyes to him and behold him crown'd,
    A deathless face.

"On the mountains of memory, by the world's well-springs,
    In all men's eyes,
Where the light of the life of him is on all past things,
    Death only dies.

"Not the light that was quench'd for us, nor the deeds that were,
    Nor the ancient days,
Nor the sorrows not sorrowful, nor the face most fair
    Of perfect praise."

So the angel of Italy's resurrection said,
    So yet he saith;
So the son of her suffering, that from breasts nigh dead
    Drew life, not death.

That the pavement of Golgotha should be white as snow,
    Not red, but white;
That the waters of Babylon should no longer flow,
    And men see light.

Love and Sleep

Lying asleep between the strokes of night
    I saw my love lean over my sad bed,
    Pale as the duskiest lily's leaf or head,
Smooth-skinned and dark, with bare throat made to bite,
Too wan for blushing and too warm for white,
    But perfect-coloured without white or red.
    And her lips opened amorously, and said —
I wist not what, saving one word — Delight.
And all her face was honey to my mouth,
    And all her body pasture to mine eyes;
        The long lithe arms and hotter hands than fire,
The quivering flanks, hair smelling of the south,
    The bright light feet, the splendid supple thighs
        And glittering eyelids of my soul's desire.

Child's Song

What is gold worth, say,
Worth for work or play,
Worth to keep or pay,
Hide or throw away,
    Hope about or fear?
What is love worth, pray?
    Worth a tear?

Golden on the mould
Lie the dead leaves roll'd
Of the wet woods old,
Yellow leaves and cold,
    Woods without a dove;
Gold is worth but gold;
    Love's worth love.

A Ballad of Life

I found in dreams a place of wind and flowers,
    Full of sweet trees and color of glad grass,
    In midst whereof there was
A lady clothed like summer with sweet hours.
Her beauty, fervent as a fiery moon,
    Made my blood burn and swoon
    Like a flame rained upon.
Sorrow had filled her shaken eyelids' blue,
And her mouth's sad red heavy rose all through
    Seemed sad with glad things gone.

She held a little cithern by the strings,
    Shaped heartwise, stung with subtle-colored hair
    Of some dead lute player
That in dead years had done delicious things.
The seven strings were named accordingly:
    The first string charity,
    The second tenderness;
The rest were pleasure, sorrow, sleep, and sin,
And loving-kindness, that is pity's kin
    And is most pitiless.

There were three men with her, each garmented
   With gold and shod with gold upon the feet;
   And with plucked ears of wheat
The first man's hair was wound upon his head.
His face was red, and his mouth curled and sad;
   All his gold garment had
      Pale stains of dust and rust.
A riven hood was pulled across his eyes;
The token of him being upon this wise
      Made for a sign of Lust.

The next was Shame, with hollow heavy face
   Colored like green wood when flame kindles it.
   He hath such feeble feet
They may not well endure in any place.
His face was full of gray old miseries,
   And all his blood's increase
      Was even increase of pain.
The last was Fear, that is akin to Death;
He is Shame's friend, and always as Shame saith
      Fear answers him again.

My soul said in me: This is marvelous,
   Seeing the air's face is not so delicate
   Nor the sun's grace so great,
If sin and she be kin or amorous.
And seeing where maidens served her on their knees,
   I bade one crave of these
      To know the cause thereof.
Then Fear said: I am Pity that was dead.
And Shame said: I am Sorrow comforted.
      And Lust said: I am Love.

Thereat her hands began a lute-playing
   And her sweet mouth a song in a strange tongue;
   And all the while she sung
There was no sound but long tears following
Long tears upon men's faces, waxen white
   With extreme sad delight.
      But those three following men
Became as men raised up among the dead;
Great glad mouths open and fair cheeks made red
      With child's blood come again.

Then I said: Now assuredly I see
  My lady is perfect, and transfigureth
  All sin and sorrow and death,
Making them fair as her own eyelids be,
Or lips wherein my whole soul's life abides;
    Or as her sweet white sides
      And bosom carved to kiss.
Now therefore, if her pity further me,
Doubtless for her sake all my days shall be
      As righteous as she is.

Forth, ballad, and take roses in both arms,
  Even till the top rose touch thee in the throat
Where the least thornprick harms;
  And girdled in thy golden singing-coat,
Come thou before my lady and say this:
Borgia, thy gold hair's color burns in me,
  Thy mouth makes beat my blood in feverish rimes;
Therefore so many as these roses be,
  Kiss me so many times.
Then it may be, seeing how sweet she is,
  That she will stoop herself none otherwise
    Than a blown vine-branch doth,
And kiss thee with soft laughter on thine eyes,
  Ballad, and on thy mouth.

A Ballad of Death

Kneel down, fair Love, and fill thyself with tears,
  Girdle thyself with sighing for a girth
  Upon the sides of mirth,
Cover thy lips and eyelids, let thine ears
  Be filled with rumor of people sorrowing;
Make thee soft raiment out of woven sighs
  Upon the flesh to cleave,
Set pains therein and many a grievous thing,
And many sorrows after each his wise
For armlet and for gorget and for sleeve.

O Love's lute heard about the lands of death,
  Left hanged upon the trees that were therein;
  O Love and Time and Sin,

Three singing mouths that mourn now underbreath,
Three lovers, each one evil spoken of;
O smitten lips wherethrough this voice of mine
Came softer with her praise;
Abide a little for our lady's love.
The kisses of her mouth were more than wine,
And more than peace the passage of her days.

O Love, thou knowest if she were good to see.
O Time, thou shalt not find in any land,
Till, cast out of thine hand,
The sunlight and the moonlight fail from thee,
Another woman fashioned like as this.
O sin, thou knowest that all thy shame in her
Was made a goodly thing;
Yea, she caught Shame and shamed him with her kiss,
With her fair kiss, and lips much lovelier
Than lips of amorous roses in late spring.

By night there stood over against my bed
Queen Venus with a hood striped gold and black,
Both sides drawn fully back
From brows wherein the sad blood failed of red,
And temples drained of purple and full of death.
Her curled hair had the wave of sea-water
And the sea's gold in it.
Her eyes were as a dove's that sickeneth.
Strewn dust of gold she had shed over her,
And pearl and purple and amber on her feet.

Upon her raiment of dyed sendaline
Were painted all the secret ways of love
And covered things thereof,
That hold delight as grape-flowers hold their wine;
Red mouths of maidens and red feet of doves,
And brides that kept within the bride-chamber
Their garment of soft shame,
And weeping faces of the wearied loves
That swoon in sleep and awake wearier,
With heat of lips and hair shed out like flame.

The tears that through her eyelids fell on me
Made mine own bitter where they ran between
As blood had fallen therein,
She saying: Arise, lift up thine eyes and see
If any glad thing be or any good
Now the best thing is taken forth of us;
Even she to whom all praise
Was as one flower in a great multitude,
One glorious flower of many and glorious,
One day found gracious among many days;

Even she whose handmaiden was Love—to whom
At kissing times across her stateliest bed
Kings bowed themselves and shed
Pale wine, and honey with the honeycomb,
And spikenard bruised for a burnt-offering;
Even she between whose lips the kiss became
As fire and frankincense;
Whose hair was as gold raiment on a king,
Whose eyes were as the morning purged with flame,
Whose eyelids as sweet savor issuing thence.

Then I beheld, and lo, on the other side
My lady's likeness crowned and robed and dead.
Sweet still, but now not red,
Was the shut mouth whereby men lived and died.
And sweet, but emptied of the blood's blue shade,
The great curled eyelids that withheld her eyes.
And sweet, but like spoilt gold,
The weight of color in her tresses weighed.
And sweet, but as a vesture with new dyes,
The body that was clothed with love of old.

Ah! that my tears filled all her woven hair
And all the hollow bosom of her gown—
Ah! that my tears ran down
Even to the place where many kisses were,
Even where her parted breast-flowers have place,
Even where they are cloven apart—who knows not this?
Ah! the flowers cleave apart

And their sweet fills the tender interspace;
Ah! the leaves grown thereof were things to kiss
Ere their fine gold was tarnished at the heart.

Ah! in the days when God did good to me,
Each part about her was a righteous thing;
Her mouth an almsgiving,
The glory of her garments charity,
The beauty of her bosom a good deed,
In the good days when God kept sight of us;
Love lay upon her eyes,
And on that hair whereof the world takes heed;
And all her body was more virtuous
Than souls of women fashioned otherwise.

Now, ballad, gather poppies in thine hands
And sheaves of briar and many rusted sheaves
Rain-rotten in rank lands,
Waste marigold and late unhappy leaves
And grass that fades ere any of it be mown,
And when thy bosom is filled full thereof
Seek out Death's face ere the light altereth,
And say: "My master that was thrall to Love
Is become thrall to Death."
Bow down before him, ballad, sigh and groan,
But make no sojourn in thy outgoing;
For haply it may be
That when thy feet return at evening
Death shall come in with thee.

Laus Veneris

Asleep or waking is it? for her neck,
Kissed over close, wears yet a purple speck,
    Wherein the pained blood falters and goes out;
Soft, and stung softly—fairer for a fleck.

But though my lips shut sucking on the place,
There is no vein at work upon her face;
    Her eyelids are so peaceable, no doubt
Deep sleep has warmed her blood through all its ways.

Lo, this is she that was the world's delight;
The old grey years were parcels of her might;
   The strewings of the ways wherein she trod
Were the twain seasons of the day and night.

Lo, she was thus when her clear limbs enticed
All lips that now grow sad with kissing Christ,
   Stained with blood fallen from the feet of God,
The feet and hands whereat our souls were priced.

Alas, Lord, surely thou art great and fair.
But lo her wonderfully woven hair!
   And thou didst heal us with thy piteous kiss;
But see now, Lord; her mouth is lovelier.

She is right fair; what hath she done to thee?
Nay, fair Lord Christ, lift up thine eyes and see;
   Had now thy mother such a lip—like this?
Thou knowest how sweet a thing it is to me.

Inside the Horsel here the air is hot;
Right little peace one hath for it, God wot;
   The scented dusty daylight burns the air,
And my heart chokes me till I hear it not.

Behold, my Venus, my soul's body, lies
With my love laid upon her garment-wise,
   Feeling my love in all her limbs and hair
And shed between her eyelids through her eyes.

She holds my heart in her sweet open hands
Hanging asleep; hard by her head there stands,
   Crowned with gilt thorns and clothed with flesh like fire,
Love, wan as foam blown up the salt burnt sands—

Hot as the brackish waifs of yellow spume
That shift and steam—loose clots of arid fume
   From the sea's panting mouth of dry desire;
There stands he, like one labouring at a loom.

The warp holds fast across; and every thread
That makes the woof up has dry specks of red;

Always the shuttle cleaves clean through, and he
Weaves with the hair of many a ruined head.

Love is not glad nor sorry, as I deem;
Labouring he dreams, and labours in the dream,
   Till when the spool is finished, lo, I see
His web, reeled off, curls and goes out like steam.

Night falls like fire; the heavy lights run low,
And as they drop, my blood and body so
   Shake as the flame shakes, full of days and hours
That sleep not neither weep they as they go.

Ah yet would God this flesh of mine might be
Where air might wash and long leaves cover me,
   Where tides of grass break into foam of flowers,
Or where the wind's feet shine along the sea.

Ah yet would God that stems and roots were bred
Out of my weary body and my head,
   That sleep were sealed upon me with a seal,
And I were as the least of all his dead.

Would God my blood were dew to feed the grass,
Mine ears made deaf and mine eyes blind as glass,
   My body broken as a turning wheel,
And my mouth stricken ere it saith Alas!

Ah God, that love were as a flower or flame,
That life were as the naming of a name,
   That death were not more pitiful than desire,
That these things were not one thing and the same!

Behold now, surely somewhere there is death:
For each man hath some space of years, he saith.
   A little space of time ere time expire,
A little day, a little way of breath.

And lo, between the sundawn and the sun,
His day's work and his night's work are undone;
   And lo, between the nightfall and the light,
He is not, and none knoweth of such an one.

Ah God, that I were as all souls that be,
As any herb or leaf of any tree,
  As men that toil through hours of labouring night,
As bones of men under the deep sharp sea.

Outside it must be winter among men;
For at the gold bars of the gates again
  I heard all night and all the hours of it,
The wind's wet wings and fingers drip with rain.

Knights gather, riding sharp for cold; I know
The ways and woods are strangled with the snow;
  And with short song the maidens spin and sit
Until Christ's birthnight, lily-like, arow.

The scent and shadow shed about me make
The very soul in all my senses ache;
  The hot hard night is fed upon my breath,
And sleep beholds me from afar awake.

Alas, but surely where the hills grow deep,
Or where the wild ways of the sea are steep,
  Or in strange places somewhere there is death,
And on death's face the scattered hair of sleep.

There lover-like with lips and limbs that meet
They lie, they pluck sweet fruit of life and eat;
  But me the hot and hungry days devour,
And in my mouth no fruit of theirs is sweet.

No fruit of theirs, but fruit of my desire,
For her love's sake whose lips through mine respire;
  Her eyelids on her eyes like flower on flower,
Mine eyelids on mine eyes like fire on fire.

So lie we, not as sleep that lies by death,
With heavy kisses and with happy breath;
  Not as man lies by woman, when the bride
Laughs low for love's sake and the words he saith.

For she lies, laughing low with love; she lies
And turns his kisses on her lips to sighs,

To sighing sound of lips unsatisfied,
And the sweet tears are tender with her eyes.

Ah, not as they, but as the souls that were
Slain in the old time, having found her fair;
    Who, sleeping with her lips upon their eyes,
Heard sudden serpents hiss across her hair.

Their blood runs round the roots of time like rain:
She casts them forth and gathers them again;
    With nerve and bone she weaves and multiplies
Exceeding pleasure out of extreme pain.

Her little chambers drip with flower-like red,
Her girdles, and the chaplets of her head,
    Her armlets and her anklets; with her feet,
She tramples all that winepress of the dead.

Her gateways smoke with fume of flowers and fires,
With loves burnt out and unassuaged desires;
    Between her lips the stream of them is sweet,
The languor in her ears of many lyres.

Her beds are full of perfume and sad sound,
Her doors are made with music and barred round
    With sighing and with laughter and with tears,
With tears whereby strong souls of men are bound.

There is the knight Adonis that was slain;
With flesh and blood she chains him for a chain;
    The body and the spirit in her ears
Cry, for her lips divide him vein by vein.

Yea, all she slayeth; yea, every man save me;
Me, love, thy lover that must cleave to thee
    Till the ending of the days and ways of earth,
The shaking of the sources of the sea.

Me, most forsaken of all souls that fell;
Me, satiated with things insatiable;
    Me, for whose sake the extreme hell makes mirth,
Yea, laughter kindles at the heart of hell.

Alas thy beauty! for thy mouth's sweet sake
My soul is bitter to me, my limbs quake
   As water, as the flesh of men that weep,
As their heart's vein whose heart goes nigh to break.

Ah God, that sleep with flower-sweet fingertips
Would crush the fruit of death upon my lips;
   Ah God, that death would tread the grapes of sleep
And wring their juice upon me as it drips.

There is no change of cheer for many days,
But change of chimes high up in the air, that sways
   Rung by the running fingers of the wind;
And singing sorrows heard on hidden ways.

Day smiteth day in twain, night sundereth night,
And on mine eyes the dark sits as the light;
   Yea, Lord, thou knowest I know not, having sinned,
If heaven be clean or unclean in thy sight.

Yea, as if earth were sprinkled over me,
Such chafed harsh earth as chokes a sandy sea,
   Each pore doth yearn, and the dried blood thereof
Gasps by sick fits, my heart swims heavily,

There is a feverish famine in my veins;
Below her bosom, where a crushed grape stains
   The white and blue, there my lips caught and clove
An hour since, and what mark of me remains?

I dare not always touch her, lest the kiss
Leave my lips charred. Yea, Lord, a little bliss,
   Brief bitter bliss, one hath for a great sin;
Nathless thou knowest how sweet a thing it is.

Sin, is it sin whereby men's souls are thrust
Into the pit? yet had I a good trust
   To save my soul before it slipped therein,
Trod under by the fire-shod feet of lust.

For if mine eyes fail and my soul takes breath,
I look between the iron sides of death

Into sad hell where all sweet love hath end,
All but the pain that never finisheth.

There are the naked faces of great kings,
The singing folk with all their lute-playings;
    There when one cometh he shall have to friend
The grave that covets and the worm that clings.

There sit the knights that were so great of hand,
The ladies that were queens of fair green land,
    Grown grey and black now, brought unto the dust,
Soiled, without raiment, clad about with sand.

There is one end for all of them; they sit
Naked and sad, they drink the dregs of it,
    Trodden as grapes in the wine-press of lust,
Trampled and trodden by their fiery feet.

I see the marvellous mouth whereby there fell
Cities and people whom the gods loved well,
    Yet for her sake on them the fire gat hold,
And for their sakes on her the fire of hell.

And softer than the Egyptian lote-leaf is,
The queen whose face was worth the world to kiss,
    Wearing at breast a suckling snake of gold;
And large pale lips of strong Semiramis,

Curled like a tiger's that curl back to feed;
Red only where the last kiss made them bleed;
    Her hair most thick with many a carven gem,
Deep in the mane, great-chested, like a steed.

Yea, with red sin the faces of them shine;
But in all these there was no sin like mine;
    No, not in all the strange great sins of them
That made the wine-press froth and foam with wine.

For I was of Christ's choosing, I God's knight,
No blinkard heathen stumbling for scant light;
    I can well see, for all the dusty days
Gone past, the clean great time of goodly fight.

I smell the breathing battle sharp with blows,
With shriek of shafts and snapping short of bows;
   The fair pure sword smites out in subtle ways,
Sounds and long lights are shed between the rows

Of beautiful mailed men; the edged light slips,
Most like a snake that takes short breath and dips
   Sharp from the beautifully bending head,
With all its gracious body lithe as lips

That curl in touching you; right in this wise
My sword doth, seeming fire in mine own eyes,
   Leaving all colours in them brown and red
And flecked with death; then the keen breaths like sighs,

The caught-up choked dry laughters following them,
When all the fighting face is grown a flame
   For pleasure, and the pulse that stuns the ears,
And the heart's gladness of the goodly game.

Let me think yet a little; I do know
These things were sweet, but sweet such years ago,
   Their savour is all turned now into tears;
Yea, ten years since, where the blue ripples blow,

The blue curled eddies of the blowing Rhine,
I felt the sharp wind shaking grass and vine
   Touch my blood, too, and sting me with delight
Through all this waste and weary body of mine

That never feels clear air; right gladly then
I rode alone, a great way off my men,
   And heard the chiming bridle smite and smite.
And gave each rhyme thereof some rhyme again,

Till my song shifted to that iron one;
Seeing there rode up between me and the sun
   Some certain of my foe's men, for his three
White wolves across their painted coats did run.

The first red-bearded, with square-cheeks—alack,
I made my knave's blood turn his beard to black;

The slaying of him was a joy to see:
Perchance, too, when at night he came not back,

Some woman fell a-weeping, whom this thief
Would beat when he had drunken; yet small grief
　　Hath any for the ridding of such knaves;
Yea, if one wept, I doubt her teen was brief.

This bitter love is sorrow in all lands,
Draining of eyelids, wringing of drenched hands,
　　Sighing of hearts and filling up of graves;
A sign across the head of the world he stands,

As one that hath a plague-mark on his brows;
Dust and spilt blood do track him to his house
　　Down under earth; sweet smells of lip and cheek,
Like a sweet snake's breath made more poisonous

With chewing of some perfumed deadly grass,
Are shed all round his passage if he pass,
　　And their quenched savour leaves the whole soul weak,
Sick with keen guessing whence the perfume was.

As one who hidden in deep sedge and reeds
Smells the rare scent made where a panther feeds,
　　And tracking ever slotwise the warm smell
Is snapped upon by the sweet mouth and bleeds,

His head far down the hot sweet throat of her—
So one tracks love, whose breath is deadlier,
　　And lo, one springe and you are fast in hell,
Fast as the gin's grip of a wayfarer.

I think now, as the heavy hours decease
One after one, and bitter thoughts increase
　　One upon one, of all sweet finished things;
The breaking of the battle; the long peace

Wherein we sat clothed softly, each man's hair
Crowned with green leaves beneath white hoods of vair;
　　The sounds of sharp spears at great tourneyings,
And noise of singing in the late sweet air.

I sang of love, too, knowing nought thereof;
"Sweeter," I said, "the little laugh of love
    Than tears out of the eyes of Magdalen,
Or any fallen feather of the Dove.

"The broken little laugh that spoils a kiss,
The ache of purple pulses, and the bliss
    Of blinded eyelids that expanded again—
Love draws them open with those lips of his,

"Lips that cling hard till the kissed face has grown
Of one same fire and colour with their own;
    Then ere one sleep, appeased with sacrifice,
Where his lips wounded, there his lips atone."

I sang these things long since and knew them not;
"Lo, here is love, or there is love, God wot,
    This man and that finds favour in his eyes,"
I said, "but I, what guerdon have I got?

"The dust of praise that is blown everywhere
In all men's faces with the common air;
    The bay-leaf that wants chafing to be sweet
Before they wind it in a singer's hair."

So that one dawn I rode forth sorrowing;
I had no hope but of some evil thing,
    And so rode slowly past the windy wheat,
And past the vineyard and the water-spring,

Up to the Horsel. A great elder-tree
Held back its heaps of flowers to let me see
    The ripe tall grass, and one that walked therein,
Naked, with hair shed over to the knee.

She walked between the blossom and the grass;
I knew the beauty of her, what she was,
    The beauty of her body and her sin,
And in my flesh the sin of hers, alas!

Alas! for sorrow is all the end of this.
O sad kissed mouth, how sorrowful it is!

O breast whereat some suckling sorrow clings,
Red with the bitter blossom of a kiss!

Ah, with blind lips I felt for you, and found
About my neck your hands and hair enwound,
    The hands that stifle and the hair that stings,
I felt them fasten sharply without sound.

Yea, for my sin I had great store of bliss:
Rise up, make answer for me, let thy kiss
    Seal my lips hard from speaking of my sin,
Lest one go mad to hear how sweet it is.

Yet I waxed faint with fume of barren bowers,
And murmuring of the heavy-headed hours;
    And let the dove's beak fret and peck within
My lips in vain, and Love shed fruitless flowers,

So that God looked upon me when your hands
Were hot about me; yea, God brake my bands
    To save my soul alive, and I came forth
Like a man blind and naked in strange lands

That hears men laugh and weep, and knows not whence
Nor wherefore, but is broken in his sense;
    Howbeit I met folk riding from the north
Towards Rome, to purge them of their souls' offence,

And rode with them, and spake to none; the day
Stunned me like lights upon some wizard way,
    And ate like fire mine eyes and mine eyesight;
So rode I, hearing all these chant and pray,

And marvelled; till before us rose and fell
White cursed hills, like outer skirts of hell
    Seen where men's eyes look through the day to night,
Like a jagged shell's lips, harsh, untunable,

Blown in between by devils' wrangling breath;
Nathless we won well past that hell and death,
    Down to the sweet land where all airs are good,
Even unto Rome where God's grace tarrieth.

Then came each man and worshipped at his knees
Who in the Lord God's likeness bears the keys
   To bind or loose, and called on Christ's shed blood,
And so the sweet-souled father gave him ease.

But when I came I fell down at his feet,
Saying, "Father, though the Lord's blood be right sweet,
   The spot it takes not off the panther's skin,
Nor shall an Ethiop's stain be bleached with it.

"Lo, I have sinned and have spat out at God,
Wherefore his hand is heavier and his rod
   More sharp because of mine exceeding sin,
And all his raiment redder than bright blood

"Before mine eyes; yea, for my sake I wot
The heat of hell is waxen seven times hot
   Through my great sin." Then spake he some sweet word,
Giving me cheer; which thing availed me not;

Yea, scarce I wist if such indeed were said;
For when I ceased—lo, as one newly dead
   Who hears a great cry out of hell, I heard
The crying of his voice across my head.

"Until this dry shred staff, that hath no whit
Of leaf nor bark, bear blossom and smell sweet,
   Seek thou not any mercy in God's sight,
For so long shalt thou be cast out from it."

Yea, what if dried-up stems wax red and green,
Shall that thing be which is not nor has been?
   Yea, what if sapless bark wax green and white,
Shall any good fruit grow upon my sin?

Nay, though sweet fruit were plucked of a dry tree,
And though men drew sweet waters of the sea,
   There should not grow sweet leaves on this dead stem,
This waste wan body and shaken soul of me.

Yea, though God search it warily enough,
There is not one sound thing in all thereof;

Though he search all my veins through, searching them
He shall find nothing whole therein but love.

For I came home right heavy, with small cheer,
And lo my love, mine own soul's heart, more dear
    Than mine own soul, more beautiful than God,
Who hath my being between the hands of her—

Fair still, but fair for no man saving me,
As when she came out of the naked sea
    Making the foam as fire whereon she trod,
And as the inner flower of fire was she.

Yea, she laid hold upon me, and her mouth
Clove unto mine as soul to body doth,
    And, laughing, made her lips luxurious;
Her hair had smells of all the sunburnt south,

Strange spice and flower, strange savour of crushed fruit,
And perfume the swart kings tread underfoot
    For pleasure when their minds wax amorous,
Charred frankincense and grated sandal-root.

And I forgot fear and all weary things,
All ended prayers and perished thanksgivings,
    Feeling her face with all her eager hair
Cleave to me, clinging as a fire that clings

To the body and to the raiment, burning them;
As after death I know that such-like flame
    Shall cleave to me for ever; yea, what care,
Albeit I burn then, having felt the same?

Ah love, there is no better life than this;
To have known love, how bitter a thing it is,
    And afterward be cast out of God's sight;
Yea, these that know not, shall they have such bliss

High up in barren heaven before his face
As we twain in the heavy-hearted place,
    Remembering love and all the dead delight,
And all that time was sweet with for a space?

For till the thunder in the trumpet be,
Soul may divide from body, but not we
   One from another; I hold thee with my hand,
I let mine eyes have all their will of thee,

I seal myself upon thee with my might,
Abiding alway out of all men's sight
   Until God loosen over sea and land
The thunder of the trumpets of the night.

      EXPLICIT LAUS VENERIS.

The Triumph of Time

Before our lives divide for ever,
   While time is with us and hands are free,
(Time, swift to fasten and swift to sever
   Hand from hand, as we stand by the sea)
I will say no word that a man might say
Whose whole life's love goes down in a day;
For this could never have been; and never,
   Though the gods and the years relent, shall be.

Is it worth a tear, is it worth an hour,
   To think of things that are well outworn?
Of fruitless husk and fugitive flower,
   The dream foregone and the deed forborne?
Though joy be done with and grief be vain,
Time shall not sever us wholly in twain;
Earth is not spoilt for a single shower;
   But the rain has ruined the ungrown corn.

It will grow not again, this fruit of my heart,
   Smitten with sunbeams, ruined with rain.
The singing seasons divide and depart,
   Winter and summer depart in twain.
It will grow not again, it is ruined at root,
The bloodlike blossom, the dull red fruit;
Though the heart yet sickens, the lips yet smart,
   With sullen savour of poisonous pain.

I have given no man of my fruit to eat;
   I trod the grapes, I have drunken the wine.
Had you eaten and drunken and found it sweet,
   This wild new growth of the corn and vine,
This wine and bread without lees or leaven,
We had grown as gods, as the gods in heaven,
Souls fair to look upon, goodly to greet,
   One splendid spirit, your soul and mine.

In the change of years, in the coil of things,
   In the clamour and rumour of life to be,
We, drinking love at the furthest springs,
   Covered with love as a covering tree,
We had grown as gods, as the gods above,
Filled from the heart to the lips with love,
Held fast in his hands, clothed warm with his wings,
   O love, my love, had you loved but me!

We had stood as the sure stars stand, and moved
   As the moon moves, loving the world; and seen
Grief collapse as a thing disproved,
   Death consume as a thing unclean.
Twain halves of a perfect heart, made fast,
Soul to soul while the years fell past;
Had you loved me once, as you have not loved;
   Had the chance been with us that has not been.

I have put my days and dreams out of mind,
   Days that are over, dreams that are done.
Though we seek life through, we shall surely find
   There is none of them clear to us now, not one.
But clear are these things: the grass and the sand,
Where, sure as the eyes reach, ever at hand,
With lips wide open and face burnt blind,
   The strong sea-daisies feast on the sun.

The low downs lean to the sea; the stream,
   One loose thin pulseless tremulous vein,
Rapid and vivid and dumb as a dream,
   Works downward, sick of the sun and the rain;
No wind is rough with the rank rare flowers;
The sweet sea, mother of loves and hours,

Shudders and shines as the grey winds gleam,
   Turning her smile to a fugitive pain.

Mother of loves that are swift to fade,
   Mother of mutable winds and hours.
A barren mother, a mother-maid,
   Cold and clean as her faint salt flowers.
I would we twain were even as she,
Lost in the night and the light of the sea,
Where faint sounds falter and wan beams wade,
   Break, and are broken, and shed into showers.

The loves and hours of the life of a man,
   They are swift and sad, being born of the sea.
Hours that rejoice and regret for a span,
   Born with a man's breath, mortal as he;
Loves that are lost ere they come to birth,
Weeds of the wave, without fruit upon earth,
I lose what I long for, save what I can,
   My love, my love, and no love for me!

It is not much that a man can save
   On the sands of life, in the straits of time,
Who swims in sight of the great third wave
   That never a swimmer shall cross or climb.
Some waif washed up with the strays and spars
That ebb-tide shows to the shore and the stars;
Weed from the water, grass from a grave,
   A broken blossom, a ruined rhyme.

There will no man do for your sake, I think,
   What I would have done for the least word said.
I had wrung life dry for your lips to drink,
   Broken it up for your daily bread:
Body for body and blood for blood,
As the flow of the full sea risen to flood
That yearns and trembles before it sink,
   I had given, and lain down for you, glad and dead.

Yea, hope at highest and all her fruit,
   And time at fullest and all his dower,
I had given you surely, and life to boot,

Were we once made one for a single hour.
But now, you are twain, you are cloven apart,
Flesh of his flesh, but heart of my heart;
And deep in one is the bitter root,
    And sweet for one is the lifelong flower.

To have died if you cared I should die for you, clung
    To my life if you bade me, played my part
As it pleased you—these were the thoughts that stung,
    The dreams that smote with a keener dart
Than shafts of love or arrows of death;
These were but as fire is, dust or breath,
Or poisonous foam on the tender tongue
    Of the little snakes that eat my heart.

I wish we were dead together to-day,
    Lost sight of, hidden away out of sight,
Clasped and clothed in the cloven clay,
    Out of the world's way, out of the light,
Out of the ages of worldly weather,
Forgotten of all men altogether,
As the world's first dead, taken wholly away,
    Made one with death, filled full of the night.

How we should slumber, how we should sleep,
    Far in the dark with the dreams and the dews!
And dreaming, grow to each other, and weep,
    Laugh low, live softly, murmur and muse;
Yea, and it may be, struck through by the dream,
Feel the dust quicken and quiver, and seem
Alive as of old to the lips, and leap
    Spirit to spirit as lovers use.

Sick dreams and sad of a dull delight;
    For what shall it profit when men are dead
To have dreamed, to have loved with the whole soul's might,
    To have looked for day when the day was fled?
Let come what will, there is one thing worth,
To have had fair love in the life upon earth:
To have held love safe till the day grew night,
    While skies had colour and lips were red.

Would I lose you now? would I take you then,
   If I lose you now that my heart has need?
And come what may after death to men,
   What thing worth this will the dead years breed?
Lose life, lose all; but at least I know,
O sweet life's love, having loved you so,
Had I reached you on earth, I should lose not again,
   In death nor life, nor in dream or deed.

Yea, I know this well: were you once sealed mine,
   Mine in the blood's beat, mine in the breath,
Mixed into me as honey in wine,
   Not time that sayeth and gainsayeth,
Nor all strong things had severed us then;
Not wrath of gods, nor wisdom of men,
Nor all things earthly, nor all divine,
   Nor joy nor sorrow, nor life nor death.

I had grown pure as the dawn and the dew,
   You had grown strong as the sun or the sea.
But none shall triumph a whole life through:
   For death is one, and the fates are three.
At the door of life, by the gate of breath,
There are worse things waiting for men than death;
Death could not sever my soul and you,
   As these have severed your soul from me.

You have chosen and clung to the chance they sent you,
   Life sweet as perfume and pure as prayer.
But will it not one day in heaven repent you?
   Will they solace you wholly, the days that were?
Will you lift up your eyes between sadness and bliss,
Meet mine, and see where the great love is,
And tremble and turn and be changed? Content you;
   The gate is strait; I shall not be there.

But you, had you chosen, had you stretched hand,
   Had you seen good such a thing were done,
I too might have stood with the souls that stand
   In the sun's sight, clothed with the light of the sun;
But who now on earth need care how I live?
Have the high gods anything left to give,

Save dust and laurels and gold and sand?
   Which gifts are goodly; but I will none.

O all fair lovers about the world,
   There is none of you, none, that shall comfort me.
My thoughts are as dead things, wrecked and whirled
   Round and round in a gulf of the sea;
And still, through the sound and the straining stream,
Through the coil and chafe, they gleam in a dream,
The bright fine lips so cruelly curled,
   And strange swift eyes where the soul sits free.

Free, without pity, withheld from woe,
   Ignorant; fair as the eyes are fair.
Would I have you change now, change at a blow,
   Startled and stricken, awake and aware?
Yea, if I could, would I have you see
My very love of you filling me,
And know my soul to the quick, as I know
   The likeness and look of your throat and hair?

I shall not change you. Nay, though I might,
   Would I change my sweet one love with a word?
I had rather your hair should change in a night,
   Clear now as the plume of a black bright bird;
Your face fail suddenly, cease, turn grey,
Die as a leaf that dies in a day.
I will keep my soul in a place out of sight,
   Far off, where the pulse of it is not heard.

Far off it walks, in a bleak blown space,
   Full of the sound of the sorrow of years.
I have woven a veil for the weeping face,
   Whose lips have drunken the wine of tears;
I have found a way for the failing feet,
A place for slumber and sorrow to meet;
There is no rumour about the place,
   Nor light, nor any that sees or hears.

I have hidden my soul out of sight, and said
   "Let none take pity upon thee, none
Comfort thy crying: for lo, thou art dead,

Lie still now, safe out of sight of the sun.
Have I not built thee a grave, and wrought
Thy grave-clothes on thee of grievous thought,
With soft spun verses and tears unshed,
    And sweet light visions of things undone?

"I have given thee garments and balm and myrrh,
    And gold, and beautiful burial things.
But thou, be at peace now, make no stir;
    Is not thy grave as a royal king's?
Fret not thyself though the end were sore;
Sleep, be patient, vex me no more.
Sleep; what hast thou to do with her?
    The eyes that weep, with the mouth that sings?"

Where the dead red leaves of the years lie rotten,
    The cold old crimes and the deeds thrown by,
The misconceived and the misbegotten,
    I would find a sin to do ere I die,
Sure to dissolve and destroy me all through,
That would set you higher in heaven, serve you
And leave you happy, when clean forgotten,
    As a dead man out of mind, am I.

Your lithe hands draw me, your face burns through me,
    I am swift to follow you, keen to see;
But love lacks might to redeem or undo me;
    As I have been, I know I shall surely be;
"What should such fellows as I do?" Nay,
My part were worse if I chose to play;
For the worst is this after all; if they knew me,
    Not a soul upon earth would pity me.

And I play not for pity of these; but you,
    If you saw with your soul what man am I,
You would praise me at least that my soul all through
    Clove to you, loathing the lives that lie;
The souls and lips that are bought and sold,
The smiles of silver and kisses of gold,
The lapdog loves that whine as they chew,
    The little lovers that curse and cry.

There are fairer women, I hear; that may be;
　　But I, that I love you and find you fair,
Who are more than fair in my eyes if they be,
　　Do the high gods know or the great gods care?
Though the swords in my heart for one were seven,
Would the iron hollow of doubtful heaven,
That knows not itself whether night-time or day be,
　　Reverberate words and a foolish prayer?

I will go back to the great sweet mother,
　　Mother and lover of men, the sea.
I will go down to her, I and none other,
　　Close with her, kiss her and mix her with me;
Cling to her, strive with her, hold her fast;
O fair white mother, in days long past
Born without sister, born without brother,
　　Set free my soul as thy soul is free.

O fair green-girdled mother of mine,
　　Sea, that art clothed with the sun and the rain,
Thy sweet hard kisses are strong like wine,
　　Thy large embraces are keen like pain.
Save me and hide me with all thy waves,
Find me one grave of thy thousand graves,
Those pure cold populous graves of thine,
　　Wrought without hand in a world without stain.

I shall sleep, and move with the moving ships,
　　Change as the winds change, veer in the tide;
My lips will feast on the foam of thy lips,
　　I shall rise with thy rising, with thee subside;
Sleep, and not know if she be, if she were,
Filled full with life to the eyes and hair,
As a rose is fulfilled to the roseleaf tips
　　With splendid summer and perfume and pride.

This woven raiment of nights and days,
　　Were it once cast off and unwound from me,
Naked and glad would I walk in thy ways,
　　Alive and aware of thy ways and thee;
Clear of the whole world, hidden at home,
Clothed with the green and crowned with the foam,
A pulse of the life of thy straits and bays,
　　A vein in the heart of the streams of the sea.

Fair mother, fed with the lives of men,
　　Thou art subtle and cruel of heart, men say.
Thou hast taken, and shalt not render again;
　　Thou art full of thy dead, and cold as they.
But death is the worst that comes of thee;
Thou art fed with our dead, O mother, O sea,
But when hast thou fed on our hearts? or when,
　　Having given us love, hast thou taken away?

O tender-hearted, O perfect lover,
　　Thy lips are bitter, and sweet thine heart.
The hopes that hurt and the dreams that hover,
　　Shall they not vanish away and apart?
But thou, thou art sure, thou art older than earth;
Thou art strong for death and fruitful of birth;
Thy depths conceal and thy gulfs discover;
　　From the first thou wert; in the end thou art.

And grief shall endure not for ever, I know.
　　As things that are not shall these things be;
We shall live through seasons of sun and of snow,
　　And none be grievous as this to me.
We shall hear, as one in a trance that hears,
The sound of time, the rhyme of the years;
Wrecked hope and passionate pain will grow
　　As tender things of a spring-tide sea,

Sea-fruit that swings in the waves that hiss,
　　Drowned gold and purple and royal rings.
And all time past, was it all for this?
　　Times unforgotten, and treasures of things?
Swift years of liking, and sweet long laughter,
That wist not well of the years thereafter
Till love woke, smitten at heart by a kiss,
　　With lips that trembled and trailing wings?

There lived a singer in France of old,
　　By the tideless dolorous midland sea.
In a land of sand and ruin and gold
　　There shone one woman, and none but she.
And finding life for her love's sake fail,
Being fain to see her, he bade set sail,
Touched land, and saw her as life grew cold,
　　And praised God, seeing; and so died he.

Died, praising God for his gift and grace:
  For she bowed down to him weeping, and said
"Live"; and her tears were shed on his face
  · Or ever the life in his face was shed
The sharp tears fell through her hair, and stung
Once, and her close lips touched him and clung
Once, and grew one with his lips for a space;
  And so drew back, and the man was dead.

O brother, the gods were good to you.
  Sleep, and be glad while the world endures.
Be well content as the years wear through;
  Give thanks for life, and the loves and lures;
Give thanks for life, O brother, and death,
For the sweet last sound of her feet, her breath,
For gifts she gave you, gracious and few,
  Tears and kisses, that lady of yours.

Rest and be glad of the gods; but I,
  How shall I praise them, or how take rest?
There is not room under all the sky
  For me that know not of worst or best,
Dream or desire of the days before,
Sweet things or bitterness, any more.
Love will not come to me now though I die,
  As love came close to you, breast to breast.

I shall never be friends again with roses;
  I shall loathe sweet tunes, where a note grown strong
Relents and recoils, and climbs and closes,
  As a wave of the sea turned back by song.
There are sounds where the soul's delight takes fire,
Face to face with its own desire;
A delight that rebels, a desire that reposes,
  I shall hate sweet music my whole life long.

The pulse of war and passion of wonder,
  The heavens that murmur, the sounds that shine,
The stars that sing and the loves that thunder,
  The music burning at heart like wine,
An armed archangel whose hands raise up
All senses mixed in the spirit's cup

Till flesh and spirit are molten in sunder—
   These things are over, and no more mine.

These were a part of the playing I heard
   Once, ere my love and my heart were at strife;
Love that sings and hath wings as a bird,
   Balm of the wound and heft of the knife.
Fairer than earth is the sea, and sleep
Than overwatching of eyes that weep,
Now time has done with his one sweet word,
   The wine and leaven of lovely life.

I shall go my ways, tread out my measure,
   Fill the days of my daily breath
With fugitive things not good to treasure,
   Do as the world doth, say as it saith;
But if we had loved each other—O sweet,
Had you felt, lying under the palms of your feet,
The heart of my heart, beating harder with pleasure
   To feel you tread it to dust and death—

Ah, had I not taken my life up and given
   All that life gives and the years let go,
The wine and honey, the balm and leaven,
   The dreams reared high and the hopes brought low?
Come life, come death, not a word be said;
Should I lose you living, and vex you dead?
I never shall tell you on earth; and in heaven
   If I cry to you then, will you hear or know?

A Cameo

There was a graven image of Desire
   Painted with red blood on a ground of gold
   Passing between the young men and the old,
And by him Pain, whose body shone like fire,
And Pleasure with gaunt hands that grasped their hire.
   Of his left wrist, with fingers clenched and cold,
   The insatiable Satiety kept hold,
Walking with feet unshod that pashed the mire;
The senses and the sorrows and the sins,
   And the strange loves that suck the breasts of Hate

Till lips and teeth bite in their sharp indenture,
Followed like beasts with flap of wings and fins.
Death stood aloof behind a gaping grate,
Upon whose lock was written *Peradventure*.

Before the Mirror

(VERSES WRITTEN UNDER A PICTURE)

Inscribed to J. A. Whistler

I

White rose in red rose-garden
  Is not so white;
Snowdrops that plead for pardon
  And pine for fright
Because the hard East blows
Over their maiden rows
  Grow not as this face grows from pale to bright.

Behind the veil, forbidden
  Shut up from sight,
Love, is there sorrow hidden,
  Is there delight?
Is joy thy dower of grief,
White rose of weary leaf,
  Late rose whose life is brief, whose loves are light?

Soft snows that hard winds harden
  Till each flake bite
Fill all the flowerless garden
  Whose flowers took flight
Long since when summer ceased,
And men rose up from feast,
  And warm west wind grew east, and warm day night.

II

"Come snow, come wind or thunder
  High up in air,
I watch my face, and wonder
  At my bright hair;

Nought else exalts or grieves
The rose at heart, that heaves
   With love of her own leaves and lips that pair.

"She knows not loves that kissed her
   She knows not where,
Art thou the ghost, my sister,
   White sister there,
Am I the ghost, who knows?
My hand, a fallen rose,
   Lies snow-white on white snows, and takes no care.

"I cannot see what pleasures
   Or what pains were;
What pale new loves and treasures
   New years will bear;
What beam will fall, what shower,
What grief or joy for dower;
   But one thing knows the flower; the flower is fair."

III
Glad, but not flushed with gladness,
   Since joys go by;
Sad, but not bent with sadness,
   Since sorrows die;
Deep in the gleaming glass
She sees all past things pass,
   And all sweet life that was lie down and lie.

There glowing ghosts of flowers
   Draw down, draw nigh;
And wings of swift spent hours
   Take flight and fly;
She sees by formless gleams,
She hears across cold streams,
   Dead mouths of many dreams that sing and sigh.

Face fallen and white throat lifted,
   With sleepless eye
She sees old loves that drifted,

> She knew not why,
> Old loves and faded fears
> Float down a stream that hears
> The flowing of all men's tears beneath the sky.

After Death

The four boards of the coffin lid
Heard all the dead man did.

The first curse was in his mouth,
Made of grave's mould and deadly drouth.

The next curse was in his head,
Made of God's work discomfited.

The next curse was in his hands,
Made out of two grave-bands.

The next curse was in his feet,
Made out of a grave-sheet.

"I had fair coins red and white,
And my name was as great light;

"I had fair clothes green and red,
And strong gold bound round my head.

"But no meat comes in my mouth,
Now I fare as the worm doth;

"And no gold binds in my hair,
Now I fare as the blind fare.

"My live thews were of great strength,
Now I am waxen a span's length;

"My live sides were full of lust,
Now are they dried with dust."

The first board spake and said:
"Is it best eating flesh or bread?"

The second answered it:
"Is wine or honey the more sweet?"

The third board spake and said:
"Is red gold worth a girl's gold head?"

The fourth made answer thus:
"All these things are as one with us."

The dead man asked of them:
"Is the green land stained brown with flame?

"Have they hewn my son for beasts to eat,
And my wife's body for beasts' meat?

"Have they boiled my maid in a brass pan,
And built a gallows to hang my man?

The boards said to him:
"This is a lewd thing that ye deem.

"Your wife has gotten a golden bed,
All the sheets are sewn with red.

"Your son has gotten a coat of silk,
The sleeves are soft as curdled milk.

"Your maid has gotten a kirtle new,
All the skirt has braids of blue.

"Your man has gotten both ring and glove,
Wrought well for eyes to love."

The dead man answered thus:
"What good gift shall God give us?"

The boards answered him anon:
"Flesh to feed hell's worm upon."

The Sundew

A little marsh-plant, yellow green,
And pricked at lip with tender red.
Tread close, and either way you tread
Some faint black water jets between
Lest you should bruise the curious head.

A live thing maybe; who shall know?
The summer knows and suffers it;
For the cool moss is thick and sweet
Each side, and saves the blossom so
That it lives out the long June heat.

The deep scent of the heather burns
About it; breathless though it be,
Bow down and worship; more than we
Is the least flower whose life returns,
Least weed renascent in the sea.

We are vexed and cumbered in earth's sight
With wants, with many memories;
These see their mother what she is,
Glad-growing, till August leave more bright
The apple-coloured cranberries.

Wind blows and bleaches the strong grass,
Blown all one way to shelter it
From trample of strayed kine, with feet
Felt heavier than the moorhen was,
Strayed up past patches of wild wheat.

You call it sundew: how it grows,
If with its colour it have breath,
If life taste sweet to it, if death
Pain its soft petal, no man knows:
Man has no sight or sense that saith.

My sundew, grown of gentle days,
In these green miles the spring begun
Thy growth ere April had half done
With the soft secret of her ways
Or June made ready for the sun.

O red-lipped mouth of marsh-flower,
I have a secret halved with thee.
The name that is love's name to me
Thou knowest, and the face of her
Who is my festival to see.

The hard sun, as thy petals knew,
Coloured the heavy moss-water:
Thou wert not worth green midsummer
Nor fit to live to August blue,
O sundew, not remembering her.

A Forsaken Garden

In a coign of the cliff between lowland and highland,
    At the sea-down's edge between windward and lee,
Walled round with rocks as an inland island,
    The ghost of a garden fronts the sea.
A girdle of brushwood and thorn encloses
    The steep square slope of the blossomless bed
Where the weeds that grew green from the graves of its roses
        Now lie dead.

The fields fall southward, abrupt and broken,
    To the low last edge of the long lone land.
If a step should sound or a word be spoken,
    Would a ghost not rise at the strange guest's hand?
So long have the grey bare walks lain guestless,
    Through branches and briers if a man make way,
He shall find no life but the sea-wind's, restless
        Night and day.

The dense hard passage is blind and stifled
    That crawls by a track none turn to climb
To the strait waste place that the years have rifled
    Of all but the thorns that are touched not of time.
The thorns he spares when the rose is taken;
    The rocks are left when he wastes the plain.
The wind that wanders, the weeds windshaken,
        These remain.

Not a flower to be pressed of the foot that falls not;
　　As the heart of a dead man the seed-plots are dry;
From the thicket of thorns whence the nightingale calls not,
　　Could she call, there were never a rose to reply.
Over the meadows that blossom and wither
　　Rings but the note of a sea-bird's song;
Only the sun and the rain come hither
　　　All year long.

The sun burns sere and the rain dishevels
　　One gaunt bleak blossom of scentless breath.
Only the wind here hovers and revels
　　In a round where life seems barren as death.
Here there was laughing of old, there was weeping,
　　Haply, of lovers none ever will I know,
Whose eyes went seaward a hundred sleeping
　　　Years ago.

Heart handfast in heart as they stood, "Look thither,"
　　Did he whisper? "look forth from the flowers to the sea;
For the foam-flowers endure when the rose-blossoms wither,
　　And men that love lightly may die—but we?"
And the same wind sang and the same waves whitened,
　　And or ever the garden's last petals were shed,
In the lips that had whispered, the eyes that had lightened,
　　　Love was dead.

Or they loved their life through, and then went whither?
　　And were one to the end—but what end who knows?
Love deep as the sea as a rose must wither,
　　As the rose-red seaweed that mocks the rose.
Shall the dead take thought for the dead to love them?
　　What love was ever as deep as a grave?
They are loveless now as the grass above them
　　　Or the wave.

All are at one now, roses and lovers,
　　Not known of the cliffs and the fields and the sea.
Not a breath of the time that has been hovers
　　In the air now soft with a summer to be.
Not a breath shall there sweeten the seasons hereafter

Of the flowers or the lovers that laugh now or weep,
When as they that are free now of weeping and laughter
    We shall sleep.

Here death may deal not again for ever;
    Here change may come not till all change end.
From the graves they have made they shall rise up never,
    Who have left nought living to ravage and rend.
Earth, stones, and thorns of the wild ground growing,
    While the sun and the rain live, these shall be;
Till a last wind's breath upon all these blowing
    Roll the sea.

Till the slow sea rise and the sheer cliff crumble,
    Till terrace and meadow the deep gulfs drink,
Till the strength of the waves of the high tides humble
    The fields that lessen, the rocks that shrink,
Here now in his triumph where all things falter,
    Stretched out on the spoils that his own hand spread,
As a god self-slain on his own strange altar,
    Death lies dead.

A Ballad of Dreamland

I hid my heart in a nest of roses,
    Out of the sun's way, hidden apart;
In a softer bed than the soft white snow's is,
    Under the roses I hid my heart.
    Why would it sleep not? why should it start,
When never a leaf of the rose-tree stirred?
    What made sleep flutter his wings and part?
Only the song of a secret bird.

Lie still, I said, for the wind's wing closes,
    And mild leaves muffle the keen sun's dart;
Lie still, for the wind on the warm sea dozes,
    And the wind is unquieter yet than thou art.
    Does a thought in thee still as a thorn's wound smart?
Does the fang still fret thee of hope deferred?
    What bids the lids of thy sleep dispart?
Only the song of a secret bird.

The green land's name that a charm encloses,
  It never was writ in the traveller's chart,
And sweet on its trees as the fruit that grows is,
  It never was sold in the merchant's mart.
  The swallows of dreams through its dim fields dart,
And sleep's are the tunes in its tree-tops heard;
  No hound's note wakens the wildwood hart,
Only the song of a secret bird.

ENVOI

In the world of dreams I have chosen my part,
  To sleep for a season and hear no word
Of true love's truth or of light love's art,
  Only the song of a secret bird.

WILLIAM MORRIS

(1834–1896)

Designer, painter, and a founder of the English Arts and Crafts movement, William Morris was also a poet, associated with the Pre-Raphaelite Brotherhood. Like others in the group, his poems reflected an abiding interest in the medieval (his *The Defence of Guenevere*, reprinted here, is considered one of the gems of Victorian poetry), and an idealized world of purity and noble sentiment. Although Swinburne remarked that Morris was always more inspired by literature than life, the latter's verse is nevertheless full of passion and drama; moreover, "…the spirit of beauty breathes in every line; a sense of music and of colour is everywhere abundant."

The Defence of Guenevere

But, knowing now that they would have her speak,
She threw her wet hair backward from her brow,
Her hand close to her mouth touching her cheek,

As though she had had there a shameful blow,
And feeling it shameful to feel ought but shame
All through her heart, yet felt her cheek burned so,

She must a little touch it; like one lame
She walked away from Gauwaine, with her head
Still lifted up; and on her cheek of flame

The tears dried quick; she stopped at last and said:
"O knights and lords, it seems but little skill
To talk of well-known things past now and dead.

"God wot I ought to say, I have done ill,
And pray you all forgiveness heartily!
Because you must be right, such great lords; still

"Listen, suppose your time were come to die,
And you were quite alone and very weak;
Yea, laid a-dying while very mightily

"The wind was ruffling up the narrow streak
Of river through your broad lands running well:
Suppose a hush should come, then some one speak:

"'One of these cloths is heaven, and one is hell,
Now choose one cloth for ever; which they be,
I will not tell you, you must somehow tell

"'Of your own strength and mightiness; here, see!'
Yea, yea, my lord, and you to ope your eyes,
At foot of your familiar bed to see

"A great God's angel standing, with such dyes,
Not known on earth, on his great wings, and hands,
Held out two ways, light from the inner skies

"Showing him well, and making his commands
Seem to be God's commands, moreover, too,
Holding within his hands the cloths on wands;

"And one of these strange choosing cloths was blue,
Wavy and long, and one cut short and red;
No man could tell the better of the two.

"After a shivering half-hour you said,
'God help! heaven's colour, the blue'; and he said, 'Hell.'
Perhaps you then would roll upon your bed,

"And cry to all good men that loved you well,
'Ah Christ! if only I had known, known, known';
Launcelot went away, then I could tell,

"Like wisest man how all things would be, moan,
And roll and hurt myself, and long to die,
And yet fear much to die for what was sown.

"Nevertheless you, O Sir Gauwaine, lie;
Whatever may have happened through these years,
God knows I speak truth, saying that you lie."

Her voice was low at first, being full of tears,
But as it cleared, it grew full loud and shrill,
Growing a windy shriek in all men's ears,

A ringing in their startled brains, until
She said that Guawaine lied, then her voice sunk,
And her great eyes began again to fill,

Though still she stood right up, and never shrunk,
But spoke on bravely, glorious lady fair!
Whatever tears her full lips may have drunk,

She stood, and seemed to think, and wrung her hair,
Spoke out at last with no more trace of shame,
With passionate twisting of her body there:

"It chanced upon a day that Launcelet came
To dwell at Arthur's court: at Christmas-time
This happened; when the heralds sung his name,

"'Son of King Ban of Benwick,' seemed to chime
Along with all the bells that rang that day,
O'er the white roofs, with little change of rhyme.

"Christmas and whitened Winter passed away,
And over me the April sunshine came,
Made very awful with black hail-clouds, yea,

"And in the Summer I grew white with flame,
And bowed my head down—Autumn, and the sick
Sure knowledge things would never be the same,

"However often Spring might be most thick
Of blossoms and buds, smote on me, and I grew
Careless of most things, let the clock tick, tick,

"To my unhappy pulse, that beat right through
My eager body; while I laughed out loud,
And let my lips curl up at false or true,

"Seemed cold and shallow without any cloud.
Behold, my judges, then the cloths were brought:
While I was dizzied thus, old thoughts would crowd,

"Belonging to the time ere I was bought
By Arthur's great name and his little love;
Must I give up for ever then, I thought,

"That which I deemed would ever round me move
Glorifying all things; for a little word,
Scarce ever meant at all, must I now prove

"Stone-cold for ever? Pray you, does the Lord
Will that all folks should be quite happy and good?
I love God now a little, if this cord

"Were broken, once for all what striving could
Make me love anything in earth or heaven?
So day by day it grew, as if one should

"Slip slowly down some path worn smooth and even,
Down to a cool sea on a summer day;
Yet still in slipping there was some small leaven

"Of stretched hands catching small stones by the way,
Until one surely reached the sea at last,
And felt strange new joy as the worn head lay

"Back with the hair like sea-weed; yea, all past
Sweat of the forehead, dryness of the lips,
Washed utterly out by the dear waves o'ercast,

"In the lone sea, far off from any ships!
Do I not know now of a day in Spring?
No minute of that wild day ever slips

"From out my memory; I hear thrushes sing,
And wheresoever I may be, straightway
Thoughts of it all come up with most fresh sting:

"I was half mad with beauty on that day,
And went without my ladies all alone,
In a quiet garden walled round every way;

"I was right joyful of that wall of stone,
That shut the flowers and trees up with the sky,
And trebled all the beauty: to the bone,

"Yea, right through to my heart, grown very shy
With weary thoughts, it pierced, and made me glad;
Exceedingly glad, and I knew verily,

"A little thing just then had made me mad;
I dared not think, as I was wont to do,
Sometimes, upon my beauty; if I had

"Held out my long hand up against the blue,
And, looking on the tenderly darken'd fingers,
Thought that by rights one ought to see quite through,

"There, see you, where the soft still light yet lingers,
Round by the edges; what should I have done,
If this had joined with yellow spotted singers,

"And startling green drawn upward by the sun?
But shouting, loosed out, see now! all my hair,
And trancedly stood watching the west wind run

"With faintest half-heard breathing sound—why there
I lose my head e'en now in doing this;
But shortly listen—In that garden fair

"Came Launcelot walking; this is true, the kiss
Wherewith we kissed in meeting that spring day,
I scarce dare talk of the remember'd bliss,

"When both our mouths went wandering in one way,
And aching sorely, met among the leaves;
Our hands being left behind strained far away.

"Never within a yard of my bright sleeves
Had Launcelot come before—and now, so nigh!
After that day why is it Guenevere grieves?

"Nevertheless you, O Sir Gauwaine, lie,
Whatever happened on through all those years,
God knows I speak truth, saying that you lie.

"Being such a lady could I weep these tears
If this were true? A great queen such as I
Having sinn'd this way, straight her conscience sears;

"And afterwards she liveth hatefully,
Slaying and poisoning, certes never weeps,—
Gauwaine be friends now, speak me lovingly.

"Do I not see how God's dear pity creeps
All through your frame, and trembles in your mouth?
Remember in what grave your mother sleeps,

"Buried in some place far down in the south,
Men are forgetting as I speak to you;
By her head sever'd in that awful drouth

"Of pity that drew Agravaine's fell blow,
I pray your pity! let me not scream out
For ever after, when the shrill winds blow

"Through half your castle-locks! let me not shout
For ever after in the winter night
When you ride out alone! in battle-rout

"Let not my rusting tears make your sword light!
Ah! God of mercy, how he turns away!
So, ever must I dress me to the fight,

"So—let God's justice work! Gauwaine, I say,
See me hew down your proofs: yea, all men know
Even as you said how Mellyagraunce one day,

"One bitter day in *la Fausse Garde,* for so
All good knights held it after, saw—
Yea, sirs, by cursed unknightly outrage; though

"You, Gauwaine, held his word without a flaw,
This Mellyagraunce saw blood upon my bed—
Whose blood then pray you? is there any law

"To make a queen say why some spots of red
Lie on her coverlet? or will you say,
'Your hands are white, lady, as when you wed,

"'Where did you bleed?' and must I stammer out, 'Nay,
I blush indeed, fair lord, only to rend
My sleeve up to my shoulder, where there lay

"'A knife-point last night': so must I defend
The honour of the Lady Guenevere?
Not so, fair lords, even if the world should end

"This very day, and you were judges here
Instead of God. Did you see Mellyagraunce
When Launcelot stood by him? what white fear

"Curdled his blood, and how his teeth did dance,
His side sink in? as my knight cried and said,
'Slayer of unarm'd men, here is a chance!

"'Setter of traps, I pray you guard your head,
By God, I am so glad to fight with you,
Stripper of ladies, that my hand feels lead

"'For driving weight; hurrah now! draw and do,
For all my wounds are moving in my breast,
And I am getting mad with waiting so.'

"He struck his hands together o'er the beast,
Who fell down flat, and grovell'd at his feet,
And groan'd at being slain so young. 'At least,'

"My knight said, 'Rise you, sir, who are so fleet
At catching ladies, half-arm'd will I fight,
My left side all uncovered!' then I weet,

"Up sprang Sir Mellyagraunce with great delight
Upon his knave's face; not until just then
Did I quite hate him, as I saw my knight

"Along the lists look to my stake and pen
With such a joyous smile, it made me sigh
From agony beneath my waist-chain, when

"The fight began, and to me they drew nigh;
Ever Sir Launcelot kept him on the right,
And traversed warily, and ever high

"And fast leapt caitiff's sword, until my knight
Sudden threw up his sword to his left hand,
Caught it, and swung it; that was all the fight,

"Except a spout of blood on the hot land;
For it was hottest summer; and I know
I wonder'd how the fire, while I should stand,

"And burn, against the heat, would quiver so,
Yards above my head; thus these matters went:
Which things were only warnings of the woe

"That fell on me. Yet Mellyagraunce was shent,
For Mellyagraunce had fought against the Lord;
Therefore, my lords, take heed lest you be blent

"With all this wickedness; say no rash word
Against me, being so beautiful; my eyes,
Wept all away the grey, may bring some sword

"To drown you in your blood; see my breast rise,
Like waves of purple sea, as here I stand;
And how my arms are moved in wonderful wise,

"Yea, also at my full heart's strong command,
See through my long throat how the words go up
In ripples to my mouth; how in my hand

"The shadow lies like wine within a cup
Of marvellously colour'd gold; yea, now
This little wind is rising, look you up,

"And wonder how the light is falling so
Within my moving tresses: will you dare,
When you have looked a little on my brow,

"To say this thing is vile? or will you care
For any plausible lies of cunning woof,
When you can see my face with no lie there

"For ever? am I not a gracious proof—
'But in your chamber Launcelot was found'—
Is there a good knight then would stand aloof,

"When a queen says with gentle queenly sound:
'O true as steel, come now and talk with me,
I love to see your step upon the ground

"'Unwavering, also well I love to see
That gracious smile light up your face, and hear
Your wonderful words, that all mean verily

"'The thing they seem to mean: good friend, so dear
To me in everything, come here to-night,
Or else the hours will pass most dull and drear;

"'If you come not, I fear this time I might
Get thinking over much of times gone by,
When I was young, and green hope was in sight:

"'For no man cares now to know why I sigh;
And no man comes to sing me pleasant songs,
Nor any brings me the sweet flowers that lie

"'So thick in the gardens; therefore one so longs
To see you, Launcelot; that we may be
Like children once again, free from all wrongs

"'Just for one night.' Did he not come to me?
What thing could keep true Launcelot away
If I said, 'Come'? there was one less than three

"In my quiet room that night, and we were gay;
Till sudden I rose up, weak, pale, and sick,
Because a bawling broke our dream up, yea,

"I looked at Launcelot's face and could not speak,
For he looked helpless too, for a little while;
Then I remembered how I tried to shriek,

"And could not, but fell down; from tile to tile
The stones they threw up rattled o'er my head
And made me dizzier; till within a while

"My maids were all about me, and my head
On Launcelot's breast was being soothed away
From its white chattering, until Launcelot said—

"By God! I will not tell you more to-day,
Judge any way you will—what matters it?
You know quite well the story of that fray,

"How Launcelot still'd their bawling, the mad fit
That caught up Gauwaine—all, all, verily,
But just that which would save me; these things flit.

"Nevertheless you, O Sir Gauwaine, lie;
Whatever may have happen'd these long years,
God knows I speak truth, saying that you lie!

"All I have said is truth, by Christ's dear tears."
She would not speak another word, but stood
Turn'd sideways; listening, like a man who hears

His brother's trumpet sounding through the wood
Of his foes' lances. She lean'd eagerly,
And gave a slight spring sometimes, as she could

At last hear something really; joyfully
Her cheek grew crimson, as the headlong speed
Of the roan charger drew all men to see,
The knight who came was Launcelot at good need.

Shameful Death

There were four of us about that bed;
    The mass-priest knelt at the side,
I and his mother stood at the head,
    Over his feet lay the bride;
We were quite sure that he was dead,
    Though his eyes were open wide.

He did not die in the night,
    He did not die in the day,
But in the morning twilight
    His spirit pass'd away,
When neither sun nor moon was bright,
    And the trees were merely grey.

He was not slain with the sword,
    Knight's axe, or the knightly spear,

Yet spoke he never a word
    After he came in here;
I cut away the cord
    From the neck of my brother dear.

He did not strike one blow,
    For the recreants came behind,
In a place where the hornbeams grow,
    A path right hard to find,
For the hornbeam boughs swing so,
    That the twilight makes it blind.

They lighted a great torch then,
    When his arms were pinion'd fast,
Sir John the knight of the Fen,
    Sir Guy of the Dolorous Blast,
With knights threescore and ten,
    Hung brave Lord Hugh at last.

I am threescore and ten,
    And my hair is all turn'd grey,
But I met Sir John of the Fen
    Long ago on a summer day,
And am glad to think of the moment when
    I took his life away.

I am threescore and ten,
    And my strength is mostly pass'd,
But long ago I and my men,
    When the sky was overcast,
And the smoke roll'd over the reeds of the fen,
    Slew Guy of the Dolorous Blast.

And now, knights all of you,
    I pray you pray for Sir Hugh,
A good knight and a true,
    And for Alice, his wife, pray too.

Summer Dawn

Pray but one prayer for me 'twixt thy closed lips,
    Think but one thought of me me up in the stars.
The summer night waneth, the morning light slips,

Faint and grey 'twixt the leaves of the aspen, betwixt the
    cloud-bars,
That are patiently waiting there for the dawn,—
    Patient and colourless, though Heaven's gold
Waits to float through them along with the sun.
Far out in the meadows, above the young corn,
    The heavy elms wait, and restless and cold,
The uneasy wind rises; the roses are dun;
Through the long twilight they pray for the dawn,
Round the lone house in the midst of the corn.
    Speak but one word to me over the corn,
    Over the tender, bow'd locks of the corn.

The Message of the March Wind

Fair now is the spring-tide, now earth lies beholding
With the eyes of a lover, the face of the sun;
Long lasteth the daylight, and hope is enfolding
The green-growing acres with increase begun.

Now sweet, sweet it is thro' the land to be straying,
'Mid the birds and the blossoms and the beasts of the field;
Love mingles with love, and no evil is weighing
On thy heart or mine, where all sorrow is heal'd.

From township to township, o'er down and by tillage,
Far, far have we wander'd and long was the day;
But now cometh eve at the end of the village,
Where over the grey wall the church riseth grey.

There is wind in the twilight; in the white road before us
The straw from the ox-yard is blowing about;
The moon's rim is rising, a star glitters o'er us,
And the vane on the spire-top is swinging in doubt.

Down there dips the highway, toward the bridge crossing over
The brook that runs on to the Thames and the sea.
Draw closer, my sweet, we are lover and lover;
This eve art thou given to gladness and me.

Shall we be glad always? Come closer and hearken:
Three fields further on, as they told me down there,

When the young moon has set, if the March sky should darken,
We might see from the hill-top the great city's glare.

Hark, the wind in the elm-boughs! from London it bloweth,
And telleth of gold, and of hope and unrest;
Of power that helps not; of wisdom that knoweth,
But teacheth not aught of the worst and the best.

Of the rich men it telleth, and strange is the story
How they have and they hanker, and grip far and wide;
And they live and they die, and the earth and its glory
Has been but a burden they scarce might abide.

Hark! the March wind again of a people is telling;
Of the life that they live there, so haggard and grim,
That if we and our love amidst them had been dwelling,
My fondness had falter'd, thy beauty grown dim.

This land we have loved in our love and our leisure,
For them hangs in heaven, high out of their reach;
The wide hills o'er the sea-plain for them have no pleasure,
The grey homes of their fathers no story to teach.

The singers have sung and the builders have builded,
The painters have fashioned their tales of delight;
For what and for whom hath the world's book been gilded,
When all is for these but the blackness of night?

How long, and for what is their patience abiding?
How long and how oft shall their story be told,
While the hope that none seeketh in darkness is hiding,
And in grief and in sorrow the world groweth old?

Come back to the inn, love, and the lights and the fire,
And the fiddler's old tune and the shuffling of feet;
For there in a while shall be rest and desire,
And there shall the morrow's uprising be sweet.

Yet, love, as we wend, the wind bloweth behind us,
And beareth the last tale it telleth to-night,
How here in the spring-tide the message shall find us;
For the hope that none seeketh is coming to light.

Like the seed of midwinter, unheeded, unperish'd,
Like the autumn-sown wheat 'neath the snow lying green,
Like the love that o'ertook us, unawares and uncherish'd,
Like the babe 'neath thy girdle that groweth unseen;

So the hope of the people now buddeth and groweth,
Rest fadeth before it, and blindness and fear;
It biddeth us learn all the wisdom it knoweth;
It hath found us and held us, and biddeth us hear:

For it beareth the message: 'Rise up on the morrow,
And go on thy ways toward the doubt and the strife;
Join hope to our hope and blend sorrow with sorrow,
And seek for men's love in the short days of life.'

But lo, the old inn, and the lights, and the fire,
And the fiddler's old tune and the shuffling of feet;
Soon for us shall be quiet and rest and desire,
And to-morrow's uprising to deeds shall be sweet.

Riding Together

For many, many days together
   The wind blew steady from the East;
For many days hot grew the weather,
   About the time of our Lady's Feast.

For many days we rode together,
   Yet met we neither friend nor foe;
Hotter and clearer grew the weather,
   Steadily did he East wind blow.

We saw the trees in the hot, bright weather,
   Clear-cut, with shadows very black,
As freely we rode on together
   With helms unlaced and bridles slack.

And often, as we rode together,
   We, looking down the green-bank'd stream,
Saw flowers in the sunny weather,
   And saw the bubble-making bream.

And in the night lay down together,
    And hung above our heads the rood,
Or watch'd night-long in the dewy weather,
    The while the moon did watch the wood.

Our spears stood bright and thick together,
    Straight out the banners stream'd behind,
As we gallop'd on in the sunny weather,
    With faces turn'd towards the wind.

Down sank our threescore spears together,
    As thick we saw the pagans ride;
His eager face in the clear fresh weather,
    Shone out that last time by my side.

Up the sweep of the bridge we dash'd together,
    It rock'd to the crash of the meeting spears,
Down rain'd the buds of the dear spring weather,
    The elm-tree flowers fell like tears.

There, as we roll'd and writhed together,
    I threw my arms above my head,
For close by my side, in the lovely weather,
    I saw him reel and fall back dead.

I and the slayer met together,
    He waited the death-stroke there in his place,
With thoughts of death, in the lovely weather,
    Gapingly mazed at my madden'd face.

Madly I fought as we fought together;
    In vain: the little Christian band
The pagans drown'd, as in stormy weather
    The river drowns low-lying land.

They bound my blood-stain'd hands together,
    They bound his corpse to nod by my side:
Then on we rode, in the bright March weather,
    With clash of cymbals did we ride.

We ride no more, no more together;
    My prison-bars are thick and strong,
I take no heed of any weather,
    The sweet Saints grant I live not long.

In Prison

Wearily, drearily,
Half the day long,
Flap the great banners
High over the stone;
Strangely and eerily
Sounds the wind's song,
Bending the banner-poles.

While, all alone,
Watching the loophole's spark,
Lie I, with life all dark,
Feet tether'd, hands fetter'd
Fast to the stone,
The grim wall, square letter'd
With prisoned men's groan.
Still strain the banner-poles
Through the wind's song
Westward the banner rolls
Over my wrong.

The Sailing of the Sword

Across the empty garden-beds,
   When the Sword went out to sea,
I scarcely saw my sisters' heads
   Bowed each beside a tree.
I could not see the castle-leads,
   When the Sword went out to sea.

Alicia wore a scarlet gown,
   When the Sword went out to sea,
But Ursula's was russet brown:
   For the mist we could not see
The scarlet roofs of the good town,
   When the Sword went out to sea.

Green holly in Alicia's hand,
   When the Sword went out to sea,
With sere oak-leaves did Ursula stand;
   O! yet alas for me!

I did but bear a peel'd white wand,
  When the Sword went out to sea.

O, russet brown and scarlet bright,
  When the Sword went out to sea,
My sisters wore; I wore but white:
  Red, brown, and white are three;
Three damozels; each had a knight,
  When the Sword went out to sea.

Sir Robert shouted loud, and said,
  When the Sword went out to sea,
"Alicia, while I see thy head,
  What shall I bring for thee?"
"O, my sweet Lord, a ruby red"—
  The Sword went out to sea.

Sir Miles said, while the sails hung down,
  When the Sword went out to sea,
"O, Ursula! while I see the town,
  What shall I bring for thee?"
"Dear knight, bring back a falcon brown"—
  The Sword went out to sea.

But my Roland, no word he said
  When the Sword went out to sea,
But only turn'd away his head;
  A quick shriek came from me:
"Come back, dear lord, to your white maid!"—
  The Sword went out to sea.

The hot sun bit the garden-beds,
  When the Sword come back from sea;
Beneath an apple-tree our heads
  Stretched out toward the sea;
Grey gleamed the thirsty castle-leads,
  When the Sword came back from sea.

Lord Robert brought a ruby red,
  When the Sword come back from sea.
He kissed Alicia on the head—
  "I am come back to thee;

'T is time, sweet love, that we were wed,
   Now the Sword is back from sea!"

Sir Miles he bore a falcon brown,
   When the Sword came back from sea;
His arms went round tall Ursula's gown—
   "What joy, O love, but thee?
Let us be wed in the good town,
   When the Sword is back from sea!"

My heart grew sick, no more afraid,
   When the Sword came back from sea;
Upon the deck a tall white maid
   Sat on Lord Roland's knee;
His chin was press'd upon her head,
   When the Sword came back from sea!"

The Haystack in the Floods

Had she come all the way for this,
To part at last without a kiss?
Yea, had she borne the dirt and rain
That her own eyes might see him slain
Beside the haystack in the floods?

Along the dripping leafless woods,
The stirrup touching either shoe,
She rode astride as troopers do;
With kirtle kilted to her knee,
To which the mud splash'd wretchedly;
And the wet dripp'd from every tree
Upon her head and heavy hair,
And on her eyelids broad and fair;
The tears and rain ran down her face.

By fits and starts they rode apace,
And very often was his place
Far off from her; he had to ride
Ahead, to see what might betide
When the roads cross'd; and sometimes, when
There rose a murmuring from his men,

Had to turn back with promises;
Ah me! she had but little ease;
And often for pure doubt and dread
She sobb'd, made giddy in the head
By the swift riding; while, for cold,
Her slender fingers scarce could hold
The wet reins; yea, and scarcely, too,
She felt the foot within her shoe
Against the stirrup: all for this,
To part at last without a kiss
Beside the haystack in the floods.

For when they near'd that old soak'd hay,
They saw across the only way
That Judas, Godmar, and the three
Red running lions dismally
Grinn'd from his pennon, under which
In one straight line along the ditch,
They counted thirty heads.

                              So then,
While Robert turn'd round to his men,
She saw at once the wretched end,
And, stooping down, tried hard to rend
Her coif the wrong way from her head,
And hid her eyes; while Robert said:
"Nay, love, 't is scarcely two to one;
At Poictiers where we made them run
So fast—why, sweet my love, good cheer,
The Gascon frontier is so near,
Nought after this."

                         But, "O," she said,
"My God! my God! I have to tread
The long way back without you; then
The court at Paris; those six men;
The gratings of the Chatelet;
The swift Seine on some rainy day
Like this, and people standing by,
And laughing, while my weak hands try
To recollect how strong men swim.
All this, or else a life with him,

For which I should be damned at last;
Would God that this next hour were past!"

He answer'd not, but cried his cry,
"St. George for Marny!" cheerily;
And laid his hand upon her rein
Alas! no man of all his train
Gave back that cheery cry again;
And, while for rage his thumb beat fast
Upon his sword-hilt, some one cast
About his neck a kerchief long,
And bound him.

                Then they went along
To Godmar; who said: "Now, Jehane,
Your lover's life is on the wane
So fast, that, if this very hour
You yield not as my paramour,
He will not see the rain leave off—
Nay, keep your tongue from gibe and scoff,
Sir Robert, or I slay you now."

She laid her hand upon her brow,
Then gazed upon the palm, as though
She thought her forehead bled, and "No,"
She said, and turn'd her head away,
As there were nothing else to say,
And everything were settled: red
Grew Godmar's face from chin to head:
"Jehane, on yonder hill there stands
My castle, guarding well my lands:
What hinders me from taking you,
And doing that I list to do
To your fair wilful body, while
Your knight lies dead?"

              A wicked smile
Wrinkled her face, her lips grew thin,
A long way out she thrust her chin:
"You know that I should strangle you
While you were sleeping; or bite through
Your throat, by God's help—ah!" she said,
"Lord Jesus, pity your poor maid!

For in such wise they hem me in,
I cannot choose but sin and sin,
Whatever happens: yet I think
They could not make me eat or drink,
And so should I just reach my rest."
"Nay, if you do not my behest,

O Jehane! though I love you well,"
Said Godmar, "would I fail to tell
All that I know?" "Foul lies," she said.
"Eh! lies, my Jehane? by God's head,
At Paris folks would deem them true!
Do you know, Jehane, they cry for you,
'Jehane the brown! Jehane the brown!
Give us Jehane to burn or drown!'—
Eh—gag me, Robert!—sweet my friend,
This were indeed a piteous end
For those long fingers, and long feet,
And long neck, and smooth shoulders sweet;
An end that few men would forget
That saw it—So, an hour yet:
Consider Jehane, which to take
Of life or death!"

                    So, scarce awake,
Dismounting, did she leave that place,
And totter some yards: with her face
Turn'd upward to the sky she lay,
Her head on a wet heap of hay,
And fell asleep: and while she slept,
And did not dream, the minutes crept
Round to the twelve again; but she,
Being waked at last, sigh'd quietly,
And strangely childlike came, and said:
"I will not." Straightway Godmar's head,
As though it hung on strong wires turn'd
Most sharply round, and his face burn'd.

For Robert—both his eyes were dry,
He could not weep, but gloomily
He seem'd to watch the rain; yea, too,
His lips were firm; he tried once more
To touch her lips; she reach'd out, sore
And vain desire so tortured them,

The poor grey lips, and now the hem
Of his sleeve brush'd them.

       With a start
Up Godmar rose, thrust them apart;
From Robert's throat he loosed the bands
Of silk and mail; with empty hands
Held out, she stood and gazed, and saw
The long bright blade without a flaw
Glide out from Godmar's sheath, his hand
In Robert's hair; she saw him bend
Back Robert's head; she saw him send
The thin steel down; the blow told well,
Right backward the knight Robert fell,
And moan'd as dogs do, being half dead,
Unwitting, as I deem: so then
Godmar turn'd grinning to his men,
Who ran, some five or six, and beat
His head to pieces at their feet.

Then Godmar turn'd again and said:
"So Jehane, the first fitte is read!
Take note, my lady, that your way
Lies backward to the Chatelet!"
She shook her head and gazed awhile
At her cold hands with a rueful smile,
As though this thing had made her mad.

This was the parting that they had
Beside the haystack in the floods.

Praise of My Lady

My lady seems of ivory,
Forehead, straight nose, and cheeks that be
Hollow'd a little mournfully.
    Beata mea Domina!

Her forehead, overshadow'd much
By bows of hair, has a wave such
As God was good to make for me.
    Beata mea Domina!

Not greatly long my lady's hair,
Nor yet with yellow colour fair,
But thick and crispèd wonderfully:
              Beata mea Domina!

Heavy to make the pale face sad,
And dark, but dead as though it had
Been forged by God most wonderfully
              —Beata mea Domina!—

Of some strange metal, thread by thread,
To stand out from my lady's head,
Not moving much to tangle me.
              Beata mea Domina!

Beneath her brows the lids fall slow,
The lashes a clear shadow throw
Where I would wish my lips to be.
              Beata mea Domina!

Her great eyes, standing far apart,
Draw up some memory from her heart,
And gaze out very mournfully;
              —Beata mea Domina!—

So beautiful and kind they are,
But most times looking out afar,
Waiting for something, not for me.
              Beata mea Domina!

I wonder if the lashes long
Are those that do her bright eyes wrong,
For always half tears seem to be
              —Beata mea Domina!—

Lurking below the underlid,
Darkening the place where they lie hid—
If they should rise and flow for me!
              Beata mea Domina!

Her full lips being made to kiss,
Curl'd up and pensive each one is;

This makes me faint to stand and see.
   Beata mea Domina!

Her lips are not contented now,
Because the hours pass so slow
Towards a sweet time: (pray for me),
   —*Beata mea Domina!*—

Nay, hold thy peace! for who can tell;
But this at least I know full well,
Her lips are parted longingly,
   —*Beata mea Domina!*—

So passionate and swift to move,
To pluck at any flying love,
That I grow faint to stand and see.
   Beata mea Domina!

Yea! there beneath them is her chin,
So fine and round, it were a sin
To feel no weaker when I see
   —*Beata mea Domina!*—

God's dealings; for with so much care
And troublous, faint lines wrought in there,
He finishes her face for me.
   Beata mea Domina!

Of her long neck what shall I say?
What things about her body's sway,
Like a knight's pennon or slim tree
   —*Beata mea Domina!*—

Set gently waving in the wind;
Or her long hands that I may find
On some day sweet to move o'er me?
   Beata mea Domina!

God pity me though, if I miss'd
The telling, how along her wrist
The veins creep, dying languidly
   —*Beata mea Domina!*—

Inside her tender palm and thin.
Now give me pardon, dear, wherein
My voice is weak and vexes thee.
            Beata mea Domina!

All men that see her any time,
I charge you straightly in this rhyme,
What, and wherever you may be,
            —*Beata mea Domina!*—

To kneel before her; as for me,
I choke and grow quite faint to see
My lady moving graciously.
            Beata mea Domina!

GEORGE MEREDITH
(1828–1909)

English novelist, poet and critic, George Meredith is widely known for such novels as *The Ordeal of Richard Feverel* and *The Egoist*–among the finest works of nineteenth-century English fiction. He was a superb poet as well, renowned for his nature poetry, whose work reveals remarkable depth of perception and insight into human psychology. His sonnet series, *Modern Love*, selections from which are printed here, is a probing and perceptive study of the relationship of husband and wife.

Lucifer in Starlight

On a starred night Prince Lucifer uprose.
Tired of his dark dominion swung the fiend
Above the rolling ball in cloud part screened,
Where sinners hugged their spectre of repose.
Poor prey to his hot fit of pride were those.
And now upon his western wing he leaned,
Now his huge bulk o'er Afric's sands careened,
Now the black planet shadowed Arctic snows.
Soaring through wider zones that pricked his scars
With memory of the old revolt from Awe,
He reached a middle height, and at the stars,
Which are the brain of heaven, he looked, and sank.
Around the ancient track marched, rank on rank,
The army of unalterable law.

Seed-Time

I

Flowers of the willow-herb are wool;
Flowers of the briar berries red;
Speeding their seed as the breeze may rule,
Flowers of the thistle loosen the thread.
Flowers of the clematis drip in beard,
Slack from the fir-tree youngly climbed;
Chaplets in air, flies foliage seared;
Heeled upon earth, lie clusters rimed.

II

Where were skies of the mantle stained
Orange and scarlet, a coat of frieze
Travels from North till day has waned,
Tattered, soaked in the ditch's dyes;
Tumbles the rook under grey or slate;
Else, enfolding us, damps to the bone;
Narrows the world to my neighbour's gate;
Paints me Life as a wheezy crone.

III

Now seems none but the spider lord;
Star in circle his web waits prey,
Silvering bush-mounds, blue brushing sward;
Slow runs the hour, swift flits the ray.
Now to this thread-shroud is he nigh,
Nigh to the tangle where wings are sealed,
He who frolicked the jewelled fly;
All is adroop on the down and the weald.

IV

Mists more lone for the sheep-bell enwrap
Nights that tardily let slip a morn
Paler than moons, and on noontide's lap
Flames dies cold, like the rose late born.
Rose born late, born withered in bud! —
I, even I, for a zenith of sun
Cry, to fulfil me, nourish my blood:
O for a day of the long light, one!

V

Master the blood, nor read by chills,
Earth admonishes: Hast thou ploughed,
Sown, reaped, harvested grain for the mills,
Thou hast the light over shadow of cloud.
Steadily eyeing, before that wail,
Animal-infant, thy mind began,
Momently nearer me: should sight fail,
Plod in the track of the husbandman.

VI

Verily now is our season of seed,
Now in our Autumn; and Earth discerns
Them that have served her in them that can read,
Glassing, where under the surface she burns,
Quick at her wheel, while the fuel, decay,
Brightens the fire of renewal: and we?
Death is the word of a bovine day,
Know you the breast of the springing To-be.

Selections *from* **Modern Love**

I

By this he knew she wept with waking eyes:
That, at his hand's light quiver by her head,
The strange low sobs that shook their common bed
Were called into her with a sharp surprise,
And strangled mute, like little gaping snakes,
Dreadfully venomous to him. She lay
Stone-still, and the long darkness flowed away
With muffled pulses. Then, as midnight makes
Her giant heart of Memory and Tears
Drink the pale drug of silence, and so beat
Sleep's heavy measure, they from head to feet
Were moveless, looking through their dead black years.
By vain regret scrawled over the blank wall.
Like sculptured effigies they might be seen
Upon their marriage-tomb, the sword between;
Each wishing for the sword that severs all.

II

It ended, and the morrow brought the task.
Her eyes were guilty gates, that let him in
By shutting all too zealous for their sin:
Each sucked a secret, and each wore a mask.
But, oh, the bitter taste her beauty had!
He sickened as at breath of poison-flowers:
A languid humour stole among the hours,
And if their smiles encountered, he went mad,
And raged deep inward, till the light was brown
Before his vision, and the world, forgot,
Looked wicked as some old dull murder-spot.
A star with lurid beams, she seemed to crown
The pit of infamy: and then again
He fainted on his vengefulness, and strove
To ape the magnanimity of love,
And smote himself, a shuddering heap of pain.

III

This was the woman; what now of the man?
But pass him. If he comes beneath a heel,
He shall be crushed until he cannot feel,
Or, being callous, haply till he can.
But he is nothing:—nothing? Only mark
The rich light striking out from her on him!
Ha! what a sense it is when her eyes swim
Across the man she singles, leaving dark
All else! Lord God, who mad'st the thing so fair,
See that I am drawn to her even now!
It cannot be such harm on her cool brow
To put a kiss? Yet if I meet him there!
But she is mine! Ah, no! I know too well
I claim a star whose light is overcast:
I claim a phantom-woman in the Past.
The hour has struck, though I heard not the bell!

V

A message from her set his brain aflame.
A world of household matters filled her mind,
Wherein he saw hypocrisy designed:

She treated him as something that is tame,
And but at other provocation bites.
Familiar was her shoulder in the glass,
Through that dark rain: yet it may come to pass
That a changed eye finds such familiar sights
More keenly tempting than new loveliness.
The "What has been" a moment seemed his own:
The splendours, mysteries, dearer because known,
Nor less divine: Love's inmost-sacredness
Called to him, 'Come!'—In his restraining start,
Eyes nurtured to be looked at scarce could see
A wave of the great waves of Destiny
Convulsed at a checked impulse of the heart.

XVI

In our old shipwrecked days there was an hour,
When in the firelight steadily aglow,
Joined slackly, we beheld the red chasm grow
Among the clicking coals. Our library-bower
That eve was left to us: and hushed we sat
As lovers to whom Time is whispering.
From sudden-opened doors we heard them sing:
The nodding elders mixed good wine with chat.
We knew we that Life's greatest treasure lay
With us, and of it was our talk. "Ah, yes!
Love dies!" I said: I never thought it less.
She yearned to me that sentence to unsay.
Then when the fire domed blackening, I found
Her cheek was salt against my kiss, and swift
Up the sharp scale of sobs her breast did lift:—
Now am I haunted by that taste! that sound!

XXXIV

Madam would speak with me. So, now it comes:
The Deluge or else Fire! She's well; she thanks
My husbandship. Our chain on silence clanks.
Time leers between, above his twiddling thumbs.
Am I quite well? Most excellent in health!
The journals, too, I diligently peruse.
Vesuvius is expected to give news:

Niagara is no noisier. By stealth
Our eyes dart scrutinizing snakes. She's glad
I'm happy, says her quivering under-lip.
"And are not you?" "How can I be?" "Take ship!
For happiness is somewhere to be had."
"Nowhere for me!" Her voice is barely heard.
I am not melted, and make no pretence.
With commonplace I freeze her, tongue and sense.
Niagara or Vesuvius is deferred.

XLV

It is the season of the sweet wild rose,
My Lady's emblem in the heart of me!
So golden-crownëd shines she gloriously,
And with that softest dream of blood she glows:
Mild as an evening heaven round Hesper bright!
I pluck the flower, and smell it, and revive
The time when in her eyes I stood alive.
I seem to look upon it out of Night.
Here's Madam, stepping hastily. Her whims
Bid her demand the flower, which I let drop.
As I proceed, I feel her sharply stop,
And crush it under heel with trembling limbs.
She joins me in a cat-like way, and talks
Of company, and even condescends
To utter laughing scandal of old friends.
These are the summer days, and these our walks.

XLVI

At last we parley: we so strangely dumb
In such a close communion! It befell
About the sounding of the Matin-bell,
And lo! her place was vacant, and the hum
Of loneliness was round me. Then I rose,
And my disordered brain did guide my foot
To that old wood where our first love-salute
Was interchanged: the source of many throes!
There did I see her, not alone. I moved
Toward her, and made proffer of my arm.
She took it simply, with no rude alarm;

And that disturbing shadow passed reproved.
I felt the pained speech coming, and declared
My firm belief in her, ere she could speak.
A ghastly morning came into her cheek,
While with a widening soul on me she stared.

XLIX

He found her by the ocean's moaning verge,
Nor any wicked change in her discerned;
And she believed his old love had returned,
Which was her exultation, and her scourge.
She took his hand, and walked with him, and seemed
The wife he sought, though shadow-like and dry.
She had one terror, lest her heart should sigh,
And tell her loudly she no longer dreamed.
She dared not say, "This is my breast: look in."
But there's a strength to help the desperate weak.
That night he learned how silence best can speak
The awful things when Pity pleads for Sin.
About the middle of the night her call
Was heard, and he came wondering to the bed.
"Now kiss me, dear! it may be, now!" she said.
Lethe had passed those lips, and he knew all.

L

Thus piteously Love closed what he begat:
The union of this ever-diverse pair!
These two were rapid falcons in a snare,
Condemned to do the flitting of the bat.
Lovers beneath the singing sky of May,
They wandered once; clear as the dew on flowers:
But they fed not on the advancing hours:
Their hearts held cravings for the buried day.
Then each applied to each that fatal knife,
Deep questioning, which probes to endless dole.
Ah, what a dusty answer gets the soul
When hot for certainties in this our life! —
In tragic hints here see what evermore
Moves dark as yonder midnight ocean's force,
Thundering like ramping hosts of warrior horse,
To throw that faint thin line upon the shore!

Index of Titles and First Lines

Index of Titles and First Lines

Titles in italics are given only when distinct from first lines.

189